Empath &
The
Narcissist

How to overcome narcissistic abuse, recover from PTSD, codependency and gaslighting manipulation.

A guide to heal childhood trauma *with* effective exercises.

Free Boundaries Workshop Inside

Raven Scott

THE EMPATH AND THE NARCISSIST

How to overcome narcissistic abuse, recover from PTSD, codependency and gaslighting manipulation. A guide to heal childhood trauma with effective exercises.

Raven Scott

Raven Scott Show Publishing

CONTENTS

FOREWORD

I know how it is to feel like you can't breathe without someone. I know the very real fear of the unknown. I know the sense of being paralyzed by fear and receiving threats from the love of your life who has turned against you because you finally chose to stand up for yourself. I cannot bear the silence any longer. The lessons and pain I endured cannot be in vain. I know there is a reason and if I can help but only one daughter, then I'm doing my duty on this Earth. We are in these vessels of bodies for a short time, and that time must not be wasted for the sake of fear.

Our future generations are depending on us to be light to those we touch. I've lived in darkness and struggled in my past every day with heart ache, isolated and alone. My prison of self-loathing and self-degrading wasted away more than ten years of my youthful life. I lost my identity to someone that wasn't pure in motives and was selfish. I lost every hobby, gift, friend, family member, and I gained one thing, a codependent & abusive relationship. By the end of the relationship, I also realized I was losing my soul.

My long journey to self-help, healing, and spiritual awakening began with the physical seeing of the dark mist that resided in my previous home with my ex. One night, after our final argument, I crawled into bed and with the light on I saw a smoky grey mist floating all around the upper portion of my bedroom. As if I was surrounded by a grey fog I could physically see the darkness surrounding me and feel it's vortex pulling me down into a dark abyss. I told myself I must get out of the dark mist and work on our relationship from a safe space. Then miraculously, that week, I was referred to a roommate and I moved out the next week.

I woke up from the matrix I had been plugged into, and my never ending journey of self discovery began.

I write this now as a woman, full of peace, joy, and contentment. Do not be fooled, I do still struggle with patterns that continue to emerge. It is like cleaning out a closet, you can address one pile at a time. I catch and observe my ego making me feel sad, and I have my moments of darkness. However, I have learned to set boundaries to fulfill my needs so that I may be the best version of myself as a mother, wife, friend, daughter, sister and role model. I am always striving to stay mindful, heart centered and tuned into my soul's worth. Since there are sensitive subject matters I have formatted this book, out of respect and protection for all parties involved, as a fictional story depicting the lessons I've learned from my pain. As I sit in my garden writing this, with my pup by my side and my beautiful kids playing, I never could imagine the amount of joy I would have on the outside of my prison of fear. I view this girl in this fictional story in a sort of out of body experience. In order to protect all parties in this sensitive memoir, none of the names used are the real names of those in my past. I am free from that state of being and it was the way of my past. I have no shame in my past and can share my lessons freely because without the mistakes and trials I experienced I wouldn't be awakened and who I am today. My desire with this book is to be the light that guides you on your journey. I am not naive to think because of this book your journey will be painless or easy, for we are given opportunities for growth through pain. However, I hope this book will shed light on your pain and fears, and you will relate to my story and learn from my mistakes. I pray you will be awakened to your soul's endless power and possibilities. You have what you need inside for joy, peace, and love in your life.

This book contains lessons, emotional exercises, meditations and tools you can apply to your life. I've included journal exercises, guided meditations and more to provide you with tools to heal, restore, and bring peace to your life.

Being that you are an empath and potentially a people pleaser, you need to work on our boundaries with narcissists, toxic people and energy drainers in order to stop the pain cycle. This is a wonderful time on your self development journey, for you to really focus on strengthening your boundaries and your inner authority. Take this time to get your free gift of The Four Ways to Set Powerful Boundaries Workshop go to https://ravenscott.show/free-workshop/

I pray this book touches your life for the better.

DEDICATION

This book is written for my
daughters, and to all the Souls of
the Divine.
Thank you for choosing me to be
your guide through this
time on Earth.

EMPATH & THE NARCISSIST:

How To Overcome Narcissistic Abuse, Recover From Ptsd, Codependency And Gaslighting Manipulation. A Guide To Heal Childhood Trauma With Effective Exercises.

1. TOXIC PATRIARCHY

How to heal childhood trauma and living up to others standards.

The wind blew through my hair, whipping my eyes, with a pitch black sky overhead, and the moon shining so bright over the flashy sports car that was careening at 90 mph like a snake through the canyon tempting fate and death.

At that moment, at age twenty, with the adrenaline running through my veins, and feeling that life was larger than I could even imagine, I thought I had arrived at the pinnacle of my fantasy.

Never in my childish dreams did I imagine my Ken doll racing Barbie along the road putting her in danger. But now I know this was just the beginning of my journey of stupid choices. Now I know this was the beginning to the end of that phase in my life. Now I know I have been jaded, a piece of pure gem pressured and roughed up. I've tried almost all of it. I've had too many crazy experiences, I do not wish to relive.

This story is all about how I lost myself and my birth given treasures, in the pursuit of my self centered desires of status, love, and acceptance. At the end when my soul couldn't take the chase anymore. I went numb and was so closed off and looked at the external world for answers. I really felt lost and forgot I shoved my amazing self, my light and treasures, deep down buried beneath. It took me years to uncover all of them. In the pursuit of my yearnings, I let all of my relationships and circumstances, even life situations, completely smother my light and hide the jewels that I had already within me. We all have beautiful treasures within ourselves; even you. Yes you, that person who feels so lost and alone, without a hope left. Our treasures are our talents and our soul. The light within us can so easily be hidden under conditioning, self hate, self doubt, trauma, and insecurities.

Do you know that old classic song?

"This little light of mine,

I'm gonna to let it shine,

This little light of mine,

I'm gonna let it shine,

Let it shine, Let it shine, Let it shine."

I was convinced and was taught that this light was the message of Christ. Now I know the external interpretation of that is false. The light is not little, it is not polite and itty bitty. It is not innocent and naive, and it is not just Christ or Christianity. It is not to be shoved down others throat or crusaded to convert masses of indigenous cultures. The light is our soul. The Light is fierce. The light is ambiguous. The light demands peace. The light breathes Source into you. You are fierce. You are power and here for a very special unique reason that is bigger than your reasoning can comprehend.

And my hope with this account is that I inspire you to start searching and looking within yourself and find your treasures and your soul's light within. To *shine* brilliant like a supernova, unapologetic, confident, and fierce like a rare white tiger.

- **Choices**

I need to note that I am not bitter or angry at my parents. I believe my soul chose this life with them for a reason. I also believe in the soul's journey of having multiple lives, reincarnating with every life allowing for a new lesson to be learned. My path as an empath through this life is Karmic, and although I wish to help you through your journey and so desire for you to not experience the pain I have endured, I know that is not realistic. We all have our Karmic journey in order for our souls to evolve, group up, and achieve a state of enlightenment. I speak of my experience in this life, and am still discovering my past lives and natal chart's planetary influences and how they relate to the lessons in this one.

- **God & Religion**

Since this story is wrapped in my soul's lessons and self discovery it is unavoidable to share about religion and spiritual concepts. After all this book will guide you in your spiritual journey. The conditioning of my religious upbringing played a key part in my story.

I want to express that I do believe in a Divine Source that guides all of the energy. The beauty in our souls having multiple lifetimes to learn and help others in the personal form is one I am convinced is true. I love the teachings of love and light being the one truth and are synonymous chords in all cultures' spiritual beliefs.

Religion is an organization that is constructed for structure and cohesiveness in a tribe. I do not condone those beliefs to be manipulated for power or political gain, or to convert others who do not believe the same. My soul aches knowing the knowledge of the Crusades, Witch Trials, Massacres of Native peoples, and global missionary efforts to "save the souls" of those "who are lost." Those indigenous were not wrong, just different, and held their own spiritual beliefs that glued their culture together. I do not refer to the Higher Source as God due the unhealthy image I interpreted in my early years. I believe there is no sex to Source, or as referred to in this book as the Universe. There are no rules or race or group of people THEY favor.

The true essence of the spirit world and physical world is that we are one. We may not physically see the spirits, Angels, and Divine, however they do exist. The veil is thick for some and thinner for others. In my experience and studies, my soul knows that there are entities always surrounding us, helping us, protecting us, and guiding us. In this book I will refer to them as Spirit Guides or Angels. I do also believe in the existence of the shadow side of the spirit world and share my first hand encounter with you in this book.

All religions are beautiful when they come from love and light and acknowledging there is a higher power greater than ourselves.

It started at the beginning...

- **Girl of privilege**

As a young girl growing up in Westchester County, with dark brown hair, brown eyes, and light skin, I was in a bubble and oblivious to how sheltered I was. By society with my light skin, and by my parents who protected me. Don't get me wrong, this is a good thing! But my karmic path had other reasons for why this (and other planetary aspects) would turn out to backfire and send me on a path of self destruction. I grew up in a small private Catholic school. I attended this tiny school my entire primary education, Kindergarten through 12th grade. We are talking small! So small my graduating class had fifty students in it. The perks of it being so small is it was a really short graduation ceremony and we didn't have to sit through too many hours of speeches and diplomas. However, the cons to it was the lack of exposure to different types of people. With the common thread of religion and minimal variety of cultures, it leant to cultural sheltering that backfired when I graduated.

So on top of being sheltered and naive, another traumatic string of events in my childhood contributed to my withdrawing from healthy relationships, and I developed low self esteem and insecurities, that I will share with you later on.

In this book I will also introduce you to Human Design and Astrology and share with you parts of my Human Design and how that played a part in my subconscious as well as the conditioning. All of us are conditioned at a very young age, and we also learn how to be and act through our mirror neurons in our brains. It is all part of our development to be a working member in a society. Our souls are here on Earth for a beautiful reason and the journey is to reawaken to what that is, and the Human Design chart and your North Node can share with you a very thematic clue as to your life's purpose, souls yearning, and your strategy for ease of flow with Source.

Go to Chapter 12 for an in depth reading on what Human Design is and how to roughly interpret your chart.

- **Conditioning**

What does that mean?

The definition of <u>condition</u> : The process of training or accustoming a person to behave in a certain way or to accept certain circumstances.

To <u>condition</u> as a verb means to have a significant influence on or determine the manner or outcome or something.

Boys and girls are raised differently. This societal conditioning separates men and women. Boys are socially conditioned to be more physical, aggressive, and competitive. Where girls are conditioned to be more communicative, nurturing, and passive. Society, culture, media, parents, teachers, and advertisers all contribute to this programming in the subtlest of ways. However we are more than just that of our biology. We are spirit and soul, it has no sex, hormones, or biology. It is pure loving energy and light. When we become aware of our true nature we understand our true selves. And releasing fear, hate, blocks and more are easier to do so.

I really had a wonderful childhood, I was loved, cherished, encouraged and raised in a stable household where both parents loved each other. I was raised and taught all the Catholic virtues of " love thy neighbor as thyself" , "Love the Lord your God with all your heart soul and mind." All the Ten Commandments. And the more traditional Virtues of "marriage is sacred and sex is something you only do with your husband." And some extreme non politically correct virtues of "you don't mix religions in a marriage" and "same sex marriage is a sin." I do not support the latter two, however they still exist in religions as something against the "tribe's" approval.

We tend to be raised in mini "village" or "bubble" communities with like minded people. There is less conflict when you surround yourself with like minded people. This is also true of the groups and channels the algorithm presents to us in our Social Media feeds. This lends also to easier conditioning and less questions by the youngsters. We are taught in a school system (public or private) where there is one method taught to all children. And all must do the work assigned. We are conditioned to succeed, work hard, and be responsible. We need to work hard and initiate our dreams. And "Just Do It" by Nike. Your parents might have pushed you toward a career that they desired for you rather than what your soul desired. And the beliefs of structured religion are quite guilt driven, in my opinion. They can be manipulative and oppressive. Individuality is not always celebrated. In the non religious school system individualism was and some cases still is labeled as disruptive, stupid, lazy, ADD, and is extra work on an already taxed system. All these systems, education, religion, and society, are trying to shove star shaped people, square shaped people, triangle shaped people, and circle shaped people into a round hole. Only a few fit into the mold while the others are forced to believe they don't fit in, are stupid, or have a disorder.

I myself was a "square" student who is designed to be patient, my go to study method if I didn't like a subject was procrastinating and memorizing things to take a test and then I would forget them directly after. (Which child doesn't do this by the way). I was smart and attended all the AP classes, and received straight A's on top of all my extracurricular activities. But non of that was directed toward a career goal. It was just to please others. I am a mutable Virgo, I strive to be perfect and constantly improve. I morphed like water into the mold that would best fit through their hole of approval. I didn't mind, yet I see how that was also not healthy on my part. I hated conflict and with Saturn in my 3rd house I had blocks in the area of communicating my feelings. My procrastination came from that fact that I didn't want to do what I wasn't interested in. This is a characteristic of a Generator. However, as a people pleaser, due to my open Solar Plexus, this is covered in Chapter 12, I always wanted to make everyone happy and do well in school.

- **It's not their fault**

Most every parent wants to make sure that their child succeeds in life, is loved, safe and sheltered from all of the bad and negative things out in the world. And that's exactly what my parents did.

They made choices to make sure that I was raised with a spiritual foundation, and made sure I had a private education and did their best to make choices that they felt at the time were best for me. I also had choices and made mistakes thinking I was making the best choice for myself at the time.

I do recall they communicated to me later in life that they made every effort to parent better than what they received. As each subsequent generation strives for. They cherished their beliefs in Christianity, and it worked for them and in turn conditioned us in the same ideas. Any parent who has found something beautiful wants to share that with their child. And others believe it's the only way to ensure their safety. I recall my grandmother, who shares the same faith, saying to me "If you don't take your kids to church, might as well take them straight to hell." As a new mom myself I thought that was extreme. As a young adult I remember being resentful that the rules of the faith were so black and white and it seemed there were no choices other than heaven and hell. The modus of operandi was "my way or the highway." There was no room for another viewpoint. For instance, they believed in Creationism directly from the Bible and not Evolution. I didn't even learn evolution in my science class in my school. I learned about it once I graduated at age eighteen. Another example is my older sister and myself were not allowed to go trick or treating until I asked one year when I was eight . Dating was avoided and I was kept busy because it may lead to sex and that is only for "wedlock". Childhood punishment for my sister, not me, was a spanking from a wooden spoon and reading of a Bible verse. This shows their journey as parents was evolving quicker than the previous generation. I do recall when we questioned the rationale of a rule, the answer when stumped was always "because I said so." We laugh about all of this now that we are adults, and I acknowledge their efforts to raise good citizens to obey the rules in society, this much is clear. And although it may have been tumultuous at times, the love was poured out and the discipline and rules were all out of love and protection.

- Question: How many of you and or your parents experienced an authoritarian upbringing?

I am sure it is 90% of us or more. But just because that's how it was, doesn't mean it is how it has to be moving forward. And our upbringing was an improvement upon our parents' upbringing.

That element of social evolution is a main theme in all our reasons for being here on Earth. To do better than the generation before, just as they did. Evolution is a slow process. The responsibility is on us to keep questioning the conditioning and rebel from it for the betterment of humanity.

- Astrological aspects affects our Psyche

I believe events in our life and circumstances can condition us and create false beliefs within our psyche. But even more strongly our astrological aspects in our natal chart, the time we were born, have a strong influence on our psyche. I struggled with self worth from the age of nine on. I really thought I was ugly, I was a loser, I was worthless. I had two major things working against me, Saturn, the ruler of Karma and blocks residing in my 3rd house of early childhood development, and my best friend felt betrayed by me and she in turn was my bully for the rest of the school year. You can look at your own 3rd house in your chart to determine how the aspects affected you. The planets residing in it have the foremost influence, then the sign in the house, and the ruler of that house is last to influence. If you do not have planets then you look at the Sign the house is in and then the ruler of that house. Saturn is in my third house and Saturn is an energy of limitations, blocks, and delays. In short, expect to struggle where you see Saturn in your chart. And don't be afraid, struggle is the most teachable energy we use to breakthrough and learn our life's lesson. Karma. So with it being in my third house I experienced a good deal of hardship in my childhood. Not as much as a child who's lost a parent (although I did in one of my past lives) or grew up in poverty always hungry. My struggle was around communication. I was shy and didn't speak much. My older sister of six years would speak for me, even to my mother. Also my sister's sun sign is in my third house. This third house has to do with childhood, first interactions as a person usually with siblings, and early learning. Saturn will also influence making friends difficult and one may feel lonely, as I did. I always felt like I didn't belong, even when people would smile and try and include me. This feeling of not feeling welcome in initial surroundings can, and did, remain a long time, all the way through high school. It's a wonder I didn't choose to switch schools in High School when I had the chance, however in the Human Design chart I have the gate of Fear of the Unknown, and I chose the familiar awkwardness. I was awkward around strangers and always sought a tender female energy to connect with in a large room of people.

In making friends I was so awkward at it, I only could develop a one on one relationship. I only had one friend at a time each year in school. I knew everyone else, but the only time I had an expanded friend group was in seventh to eighth grade. And that was only because that one friend of mine made them as friends and the social interaction with her was in a group. In 5th grade I made a best friend, we did a thing that I share in the next chapter. The guilt of my mistake and her retaliating made the false belief I was worthless govern my self esteem for decades. Saturn is all about the past, and if you're not conscious you can beat yourself up about past mistakes. My father would try and tell me "You are beautiful." I would always answer with disbelief "You have to say that because you're my dad." I always believed I wasn't worthy of love because of this betrayal and her locking in my loser status. I truly believed I was ugly, and no one would love me. I couldn't believe I had a boy ask me out when I reached age fifteen. I was grateful, and excited. I still didn't believe I was worthy and broke up with him to protect myself.

Once I met the Mr. that I mentioned in the opening that drove us 90 mph in his Porsche around winding roads in the hillsides, I had two dates total with no physical contact! Three years later when I was in my Senior Year of High School, which feels like forever at that age, this Porsche driver became my friend who then became my boyfriend. I felt so lucky and put him on such a high pedestal. He was handsome, tall, blue eyes, and prestigious in our church we met in. Little did I know he was a "cool glass of water, but he was candy coated misery." Thank you Carrie Underwood for describing the Narcissist so eloquently. I'll tell you more about this story in chapters to come since this time in my life is the main reason I am writing this book.

- Raving Raven

As a child, under the age of six, I had really big emotions and I had very big temper tantrums and the neighbors called me "Raving Raven" and I had a reputation for being very loud and boisterous when I was upset. Saturn brings blocks of communication. One can feel frustration and an inability to express themselves and fear that no one will understand your thoughts. I felt these both painfully. I had loud outbursts of frustration and anger as a young child when playing with my block friends. When there was conflict my mom would try and console me and find a solution calmly but there was no calming it down. And that seemed to put fuel to the fire and she just never seemed like she could win or help me. So she sent me to my room because I could get it all out without disturbing everyone else. And for me as the child on that end I felt so frustrated and felt lost like I didn't know how to deal with my emotions and she was at a loss for tools too, she did not know how to deal with my emotions. I will share on the Centers later, but this I now see as my open Solar Plexus Center. This Center governs the emotions. This energy center when it is open amplifies other people's emotions. We tend to be the loudest in voicing our emotions and amplify ourselves and others emotions.

So when my friends and I would have a disagreement, we all got upset, but my immature emotions and my open solar plexus amplified the emotions of the other and I was the one who shouted everyone's emotions to the roof tops. And I was conditioned to hide my emotions and remain quiet, as I raged when I amplified anger. This kind of energy can do damage inside the body. If you have a child dealing with this, what you can do is hold space for them and don't solve anything. Find an outlet for that frustration, breathe, squeeze a stress ball, exercise or stuff like that. And of course you could just hold them, if you can and acknowledge the visitor of anger. It's just a wave, and it will pass. Repeat "I know, I know." and the wave will subside quicker than resisting the anger.

It's not anything the child can "stop", so telling them to stop frustrates them more. Instead teach them to breathe and wait out the wave. Over time in holding them, and holding space for them, they will know it's just a wave and to breathe and they will deal with emotions much more elegantly as they grow older. And the episodes get shorter and shorter. It's really a matter of just feeling loved, and being seen and heard, so actually allow them to really feel deeply through those thoughts, even if it's untrue and hold and hug them. And then once the wave of emotion is stabilizing, find examples of how that situation could be resolved moving forward.

It's a huge process and it is work, especially for us open solar plexus parents. I don't know about you, but when my child is upset I feel deep anxiety and I feel their emotions ten times stronger. It takes daily mindfulness to breathe and know this fact so I can hold space and be calm while I wait out the emotional wave with my child. It took me many years to figure out that emotions are visitors. They come, they stay for a little bit and then they leave. And that's exactly what they are, and I'm just learning this now at thirty-six. It will be rewarding once you can teach yourself this first. Because a lot of times when our emotions are clouding our judgment and filling up our hormones with fight or flight, we're not able to really understand what's going on.

And our emotions have wavelengths. On the flip side of the open Solar Plexus, those who have a defined Solar Plexus have a steady wave of emotions. As children if they have the emoting gate, (gates are like energy circuits of your personality) they will have very high waves of emotion, and very low waves of emotion. You just have to do the same as the open gate child, hold space and allow them to be loved and allowed to go through the wave. Remind them and ask them if this is an ANT. Automatic Negative Thought, or a "Blue thought" and don't lecture, just help them recognize their low part of their wave and that *all* our thoughts are *not* true.

Sadness and anger are considered ugly in our society. It is probably because all of us with the open solar plexus don't want to feel those emotions ten fold. Wink wink. It triggers stress and fight or flight hormones. But if we can recognize they are ok. Stop conditioning our children to "be quiet" or "suck it up", stop covering it up and say "you're fine don't be so dramatic". That language isn't raising emotionally intelligent people, and it is very damaging. That energy should not be held in our bodies, or it will manifest in health or behavioral issues.

No matter what type you are or what centers are open or defined in your Human Design, we as parents carry a lot of stress in our bodies trying to manage everyone's emotions, schedules, educations, meals, and physical activities. The best thing to do is stop trying to control any of these. And embrace everyone's type of personality. Stress can occur if we are not being mindful and not open to being present in the moment with our loved ones. Stress not dealt with can result in unwanted yelling, emotional outbursts, depression, anxiety, panic attacks, and more physical illnesses and ailments such as muscle lock up or IBS.

As a child you learn to hide emotions because they are frowned upon, but it doesn't cure the temper, it just shoves it down. As an adult you still don't know how to communicate all that so it just kind of blows up like a big storm. And as you get older society expects that you should just figure it out and get over it. But if you don't know the tools you haven't learned to really figure out what to do with those emotions when they explode. The outbursts are going to continue as an adult. You may yell at your spouse or boyfriend or whoever you're close with. And once you have a child the burden, anxiety and stress of a mom or dad, then creates a perfect storm for your outbursts. And you find yourself yelling at your children and they cry and you feel horrible because you are the cause of their pain in that instance. You find yourself in constant battle with your partner and instead of creating a beautiful family, you have created World War III and everyone is on edge.

To stop this vicious cycle it's really a matter of developing the tools and skills to manage the stress and anxiety. And this idea is not that you have to be perfect and do all this stuff so everyone will like you. You are never free of this pressure to people please until you acknowledge you have that open solar plexus and you don't have to please others anymore.

- **Angels**

I can't even imagine how many angels were watching over me while I was in that car that could have easily crashed and we would've been instantly gone. I had blind faith in my invincibility being 20, and blind faith in a man I foolishly trusted with my life. Never would I have imagined in that moment worrying about babies and being responsible with myself to be present for them. Life is full of twists and turns like that.

Treasures Lost: Inner authority (pleasing others instead of considering my needs)

Main Human design Element at play: Open Solar Plexus - People Pleasing obedient quiet child that is afraid to stir the pot. Read more about Human Design in Chapter 12.

To dive deeper into this topic listen to Ep. 47 Rise Against Covert Narcissism on the Empath & The Narcissist Podcast.

-   HOW TO CHANGE PATRIARCHAL PATTERNS

-   *Conscious Parenting*

The most impactful way I have evolved the way I parent is being mindful and conscious. Conscious parenting is about seeing the child as another unique soul rather than someone to control and govern. I consider and call myself their guide. I give them options about their choices with their body and time. I set boundaries where they need, and encourage their uniqueness and eradicate antiquated language that will make them feel judged or categorized. For instance, one summer when my daughter was six, she wanted a boy's haircut. Instead of being afraid she didn't want to be a girl anymore, I was open and informed her how short it will be. She understood and still wanted to cut it. I did not tell her she couldn't because she was a girl. I went along and supported her experiment and haircut. She was beaming after I cut all her beautiful hair off. Dressed like a boy, with a haircut like a boy she looked cool! She felt seen, heard and supported. And while still playing with baby dolls and loving athletic activities she has taught me and whomever she meets that there is no pink definition of a girl. Girls can be cool and tough just like boys can like pink and baby dolls. She is the beautiful model of our androgenous souls.

Book: The Conscious Parent by Dr. Shefali is the woman who started the conscious parenting movement. You will find her everywhere online, YouTube, Facebook, and Instagram.

Certified Conscious Parenting Coaches are readily available now, thanks to her. They are essential to your sanity with your child and can help rewrite how you parent to evolve away from how your parents raised you.

- ASTROLOGY FOR SELF DISCOVERY

- *What influences your 3rd and 4th house of siblings and family?*

Astrology is a powerful tool to explain the energies that we all contain within us from all the planets in the solar system. Have you pulled up your natal chart? If not you can for free from several websites. I like astrology.com, astrologyuniversity.com, and astro.com. If you need help email me. ravenscottshow@gmail.com. I can help research your 3rd house and the influences it holds in it's aspects.

Each planet has a certain energy and theme. And each house contains an area of your life that planet influences and highlights. All of this is to help us grow and evolve. And if we know the energies we can conceptualize, heal and use this energy for our benefit.

You can use the tool for understanding your feelings, interactions in your relationships, your struggles, and use it as a holistic approach to your self care and wellness. I'll briefly cover the planets energies and house themes for you to get a peek into the power of this tool.

Planets

Sun is the planet of self.

Moon is the planet of emotions.

Mercury is the planet of communication and conceptualization.

Venus is the planet of love and money.

Mars is the planet of passion and action.

Jupiter is the planet of luck and expansion.

Uranus is the planet of rebellion and evolution.

Neptune is the planet of illusion and dreams.

Pluto is the planet of power and shadows.

Zodiacs

There are twelve zodiac signs in the year. As the sun passes through each zodiac, like a minute hand ticking through an hour, that defines one zodiac season. We look to the zodiac signs to shed light on our personalities, themes of a planet's influence, and insights.

ARIES IS THE ASTROLOGER'S NEW YEAR.

Aries (3/21- 4/19) characteristics are assertive, brave, carefree, direct, energetic, enterprising, hot-tempered, impatient, impulsive, individualistic, pioneering and willful. This a Fire sign that brings new beginnings, enthusiasm and passion.

Taurus (4/20 - 5/20) characteristics are creative, grounded, kindhearted, patient, methodical, practical, predictable, security emphasized, luxurious self-indulgent, sensual, steadfast, and stubborn. This is an Earth sign that embodies grounding, planning and creative projects.

Gemini (5/21 - 6/21) characteristics are adaptable, cunning, curious, dual-natured, fickle, informative, talkative, quick-witted, and youthful. This is an Air sign that is flexible and agile energy for thoughts and logic.

Cancer (6/22 - 7/22) characteristics are defensive, emotional, gentle, hospitable, indirect, sensitive, nurturing, moody, protective and empathetic. This is a Water sign that is fluid and emotionally reflective.

Leo (7/23 - 8/22) characteristics are charismatic, cheerful, courageous, dignified, dramatic, faithful, warmhearted, kind, proud, and forthright. This is a Fire sign that is dynamic energy of inspiration and enthusiasm.

Virgo (8/23 - 9/22) characteristics are analytical, anxious, critical, detailed, diligent, efficient, helpful, logical, orderly, precise, rational, tidy. This is an Earth sign that is grounded, mutable with an affinity for finessing projects.

Libra (9/23 - 10/22) characteristics are charming, diplomatic, equitable, gracious, indecisive, judicious, orderly, poised, romantic, sociable, stylish, and agile. This is an Air sign that loves new beginnings and energy of thoughts.

Scorpio (10/23 - 11/21) characteristics are brooding, complex, determined, emotional, forceful, intense, passionate, probing, regenerative, resilient, resourceful, and secretive. This is a Water sign is fluid emotional energy and sensitive and personal.

Sagittarius (11/22-12/21) characteristics are adventurous, dogmatic, exuberant, inspired, jovial, optimistic, wise, upbeat, visionary, and physically bouncy. This is a Fire sign full of dynamic energy and flexible.

Capricorn (12/22 - 1/20) characteristics are ambitious, committed, conservation oriented, disciplined, frugal, hardworking, loyal, persistent, pragmatic, structured, sarcastic, and a realist. This is an Earth energy that is grounded and practical.

Aquarius (1/21 - 2/18) characteristics are altruistic, cerebral, detached, eccentric, community minded, friendly, independent, philanthropic, progressive and rebellious. This sign is an Air sign with agile thoughts, communication, and energized alliances.

Pisces (2/19 - 3/20) characteristics are dreamy, elusive, empathetic, idealistic, imaginative, impressionable, poetic, psychic, selfless, and spiritual. This sign is a Water sign with fluid sensitivity, soulful connections, and intuition.

House Themes

Just as there are twelve zodiac signs, there are twelve houses. So when you look at your chart and look at your third and fourth house I referred to, the planets in these houses affect your lessons and themes in these areas of your life. If you do not have planets in a house, the planets opposite them in the chart give influence to the house as well as the ruling planet of that zodiac.

First House - Theme of self identity

Second House - Theme of possessions and money

Third House - Theme of communication and siblings

Fourth House - Theme of family and home

Fifth House - Theme of hobbies, pleasure, and offspring

Sixth House - Theme of health

Seventh House - Theme of partnership

Eighth House - Theme of sex

Ninth House - Theme of philosophy

Tenth House - Theme of social status & career

Eleventh House - Theme of friendships

Twelfth House - Theme of subconscious

As all of this information is outlined for you, I understand it will require more digging. Allow yourself to gain multiple perspectives, let time share and solidify your knowledge. All of this information is for you to use as a clarity tool. When you have been conditioned and confused of why you are encountering certain pains from childhood trauma, it is an onion to unfold all the layers of toxic behaviors, patterns, unsavory truth, shame, blame, and gaslighting.

This information will allow you to heal your childhood wounds through the exercises and meditations in this book. It will allow you to identify your needs and what you will continue to put up with. And draw boundaries with the behaviors and people that you are not willing to hurt you anymore. Take advantage of the journal and reflective time provided for you in the next section.

- PARENTING MANIFESTO JOURNAL

During your quiet time or devotion time, write down what your parents' parenting style was.

Identify the moments you have regretted and felt healthy shame afterwards.

What areas do you see yourself blindly repeating what you experienced as a child?

Discuss it with your partner and agree to call it out for each other when you see it. Because it is so engrained you will miss it if you rely on yourself. So many times my partner has shared with me when I am doing something I have voiced to him I didn't like about my childhood. And since I am open to change I hear him out and try to stop that moving forward. Parenting takes a village and your best chance for change is your partner.

Journal how you wished your parents would have done things with you and recognize you have the chance to set an intention to change that for your children now.

If you do not have kids or they are grown, What areas of your relationships and self do you see the negative effects of your parents or siblings actions in the past? Set intentions to love yourself better than anyone can.

Read this prayer for 21 days straight

I hereby set the intention that my healed ancestral line be restored to it's original state. Allow me to listen and guide with complete ease and abundance, knowing that the Divine is the unlimited Source of all.

Let me trust that all my own needs are always met in amazing ways and that it's safe to give love freely as my heart guides.

And equally let me feel wildly open to showing up authentically and vulnerably. Allowing me to apologize when appropriate to model healthy behavior.

Let me play when it's time to play. Discuss when it's time to discuss. And draw boundaries when it's time to teach respect and love.

May I know my own value, power and worthiness without question. So that when my child's ego battles back, I remain patient and loving.

Rescind all ancestral vows that no longer serve my highest path and purpose. Release and clear all related negative energies held at all dimensional levels of my existence.

Let all wounds that need to go, go. Let all patience and wisdom that need to come, come.

Change me into one who can fully love, forgive, and accept myself so I may show up with a full cup to guide, love, and accept my child as they are; and with all their tough emotions, *and unexpected curveballs.*

Raising a strong emotional minded person with integrity is the upmost important to me.

In the highest good of all beings, I entrust this intention to be carried out with joy. So be it. So it is. Thank you, thank you, thank you.

2. FORCES THAT DRIVE CODEPENDENCY

How to heal your self worth from bullying and learn to love yourself, raise self esteem and avoid narcissistic abuse

I can smell the dirt and feel the sweat on the hands of my classmates as we stand in a line facing our other classmates in their own line. The adrenaline rose through my blood each time "Red Rover Red Rover send - " My heart stopped for a split second, the anticipation of hearing my name. That meant I was liked, I was accepted in the tribe, I was worthy. I kept waiting, and waiting, until one more hand was left holding mine. Her name was called, she went running over. And the world and time stood still as they all knelt down on their knees in front of me barking like dogs in mockery of me.

I don't know what happened next. I froze, I was mortified, in shock. Because I knew my friend who was once my best ally orchestrated the entire event.

The bell rang and up the stairs we all went back into the classroom.

All the other students had no idea why they just did this heinous act of group bullying. It was a herd mentality game of telephone. She planned it, told her new best friend, and that girl spread the plan to all the other classmates. This one year in the fifth grade scarred my ego and self esteem until I was three decades old.

-Lollipops and Sleepovers

At the age of first boy crushes, sleepovers, and lollipops I had an unusual encounter with my best friend that ended very badly. Sally will be her alias name for privacy reasons.

Sally and I were besties. We did everything together. We played every recess, we sat next to each other at lunch, and were tight. Yeah, you know, besties at eleven. One day we came up with the idea to have a sleepover to continue our fun just as all normal girls do. She asked if I could come over and stay at her house and I was happy to. It wasn't my first sleepover, however it was the first time I had been over to *her* house. We played outside, rode bikes, and had a blast.

Then it was time for bed. We slept out in the living room on the sleeper sofa. She turned the TV on and we started talking about our boy crushes. She had the brilliant idea to pretend we were each other's boy crush. Now this wasn't my first rodeo of people convincing me it was a good idea to role play something inappropriate. Rewind to five years prior, my poor mom caught me with my pants down at age five with my friends innocently playing doctor and I was completely oblivious it was wrong. However I got the sense it was upon her reaction. This by the way is the effect of my open will center. One with an open will center amplifies others wills and desires and goes with the flow. And with my open Solar Plexus, not wanting to make anyone mad, so I wouldn't feel their anger or sadness amplified. This resulted in my becoming the "yes" girl. This lends for an easily influenced naive innocent child. Children with this combination are easily manipulated. It is important to know if your child has this. In order to have clear conversations on boundaries, and appropriate behavior. This is important for every child, but the repetition is most important for this type of people pleasing child. I didn't have the radar for the consequences of others' crazy ideas.

Back to the suspenseful part - We somehow started making out and fondling each other and then *wowza* we were doing the deed. We had done "the forbid sin." The next day when I woke up and went home, somehow we both knew it was an unspoken pact that this would remain private and to ourselves. We both knew the Catholic laws that sex before marriage was a sin let alone same sex activity.

Once I was home and a day went by, I was getting ready to go to church and be a good Catholic girl. My stomach was in knots and I felt so sick churning with this secret. It was too intense and too much for me to hold in. I was in real pain.

A side note on the Sacral Center. This is the center for me that is defined and is my authority in living my truest self. I wasn't being honest, I had broken a virtue, and I had so much guilt over it. My authority was screaming "NOOOOO." I knew what I did was wrong from my conditioning and in the eyes of God and my Catholic upbringing and it was too much for my little psyche to bear. Have you ever bought something and had buyers remorse? Ya! Kind of like that but with an activity. This activity is perfectly normal between two consenting adults no matter what the orientation.

As a child, I felt ashamed, and scared, and my stomach ache made me confused. Since I was only ten and did not yet get the birds and the bees talk I thought my stomach pain meant I was pregnant! Our innocent role playing experience was so burdensome that I broke down and told my mom. "I think I am pregnant." I sobbed to my mom. Thankfully, my mom was very kind and she reassured me it was no big deal and she explained to me that it's physically not possible to get pregnant at this age and with another girl. There was my crash course on the mini version of the birds and the bees. I remember feeling so much relief and my stomach pain immediately went away. I felt silly and embarrassed but that paled in comparison.

My mom did not chastise me. She was very kind and maybe deep down inside she was panicking. *Not again! This girl took advantage of my daughter.* She must've thought. So she handled it the best she knew. She made Sally's mother aware of what we did. ...Well throw me in that coffin and nail it while you're at it! I don't blame her, as a mother I would've done the same. Or would I? But, now my husband would probably stop me, but that's why we find a balance in our partners.

That was the death of my friendship, the death of my self esteem, and the death of my trust in friends for decades.

~It's ok mom. I forgive you. You did your best.

- **The bestie turned bully**

And Sally, with an older brother to chastise her and a strict mother, must've gotten it much worse than I did. She was so hurt by my betrayal and hated me with the passion of a thousand suns. This was our struggle. We all have them and now you know why she had the entire class bully me.

When I went to school the next day, she didn't speak to me. I wasn't to be trusted and did not exist in her eyes. And she plotted a plan to hurt me back one hundred times over.

She was my best friend who turned into my cruel bully. She made mean jokes and comments to me for the rest of the year. I received months worth of daily insults towards my looks, she called me ugly, she called me a dog, and she made a new friend who had an open will center like myself and they both would bark at me and get on their knees and bark and laugh. "You're so ugly like a dog. Woof woof. Haha" She excluded me from any recess game she was a part of. There was no escaping her because this school is so freakishly small and she was in my class of twenty students. I came home crying every day. But with Saturn blocking my communication I would not tell my mother why I cried. I was so hurt and embarrassed I didn't put two and two together.

Sally left the school the next year, I don't think she could bear it anymore either. And this girl who joined in made fun of me, her new best friend, remained at the school. Her taunts stopped without her boss. Senior year of high school she said to me, "Remember that one time, like (that is exactly how she spoke), we made fun of you. Like. What was that about? Why did we do that?" She had no idea she was amplifying the will of my friend, nor did I.

I replied, "I don't know." I had not dealt with it myself, nor reveal what really happened to a group of my peers. I wasn't able to help her process. That year during a student body retreat, all the responsibility and guilt and negative feelings of never fitting in caught up with me. I stayed in bed depressed during the entire retreat. It took me until I was thirty and Sally entered into my therapy sessions. How I ended up in a therapy session is a story for the chapters to come. But the pain from her wounds was what needed to come forward. And I needed to heal so I could move on in my life. The power of forgiveness and release is amazing.

-   Signs Of Low Self Esteem

Codependency is driven by a lack of identity.

On my spiritual journey after many years of therapy, self introspection, meditation, and denial of the harsh truth, I learned that codependency is driven by a lack of identity.

And I, myself have been diagnosed codependent. When I left my narcissistic relationship and went to therapy, she introduced me to what codependency is. I define it in more detail in a future chapter to come, but I will give you a short description here. Codependency is, this intertwined enmeshed emotional feeling. You know, being needed by somebody enabling their bad behavior, just so that you can continually be able to take care of them, to receive attention and to feel needed.

And all of that attention can be wrapped up into your identity if you have been stunted emotionally in your early developmental years. There are a few reasons, a lack of skills taught to you by your caregivers, your ego, ancestral toxic behaviors, and/or unhealed childhood trauma.

Unhealed childhood trauma shows up in one's life and relationships as fixing others, people pleasing, codependency, external validation, being needed, need to prove yourself, on high alert all the time, feel like your walking on eggshells, fear of abandonment, and tolerates abuse.

The signs that you may have low self esteem are:

1. People pleasing.

2. Lack of setting and holding boundaries.

3. Harsh self talk .

4. Lack of integrity or unwavering values.

5. Yearning for praise outside yourself.

So what drives the empath or you towards codependency and basing your self-worth on the outside influences of others? The outside event. The outside invitations, and the outside praise?

Empaths are conditioned to be codependent and seek self worth outside themselves. But that doesn't mean you cannot be free of this conditioning and rewrite your behaviors. There are three main ways life circumstances govern this toxic survival mechanism.

1. They are not provided freedom of mind and autonomy of self in the crucial formative pubescent years.

2. Childhood bullying by peer, parent, or sibling.

3. Lack of emotional tools provided by the parent / caregiver.

Freedom Of Autonomy

To understand that radical ideologies hinder emotional growth, I must define a few basic concepts.

Ideologies in psychology are defined as more or less a systematic ordering of ideas with associated doctrines, attitudes, beliefs, and symbols that together form a more or less (radical) coherent philosophy for a person, family, or group.

Radicalisation is the process through which an individual or group develops extreme political, social and religious beliefs.

Violent extremism is when a person or group uses fear, terror or violence to try and achieve change. (this can be physical, political, or emotion violence)

Sound familiar? These are all narcissistic tactics of terror for control that we will cover in chapter 6.

A cult is a group or movement held together by a shared

commitment to a charismatic leader or extreme ideology. It has a belief system that has the answers to all of life's questions and offers a special solution to be gained only by following the leader's rules.

What I've found is in my personal discovery, that the number one influence of a lack of self identity is being raised and developed in a family unit that does not allow freedom of autonomy in their formative teenage years for self-discovery.

Autonomy is: a person's ability to act on his or her own values and interests. It is having the ability to make one's own decisions independently of external control.

A parent may argue to their adult child that they did provide freedom and choices. But I would ask you, was that freedom free of judgement and guilt? I'm sure you can relate that when you are raised in a culture that nurtures perpetual threat of "sinning" and "going to hell". The guilt and shame is a formidable force that does not allow for a person's true autonomy.

Due to a strict ideology, whether it be a religion or even veganism. No organization or idea is bad if well balanced. Yet when it is extreme and from a source of close minded, extreme idealism that radicalisation can wreak serious havoc on a person's emotional development. And if they don't abide by the "cult's" rules or virtues, they are a bad person, and condemned to torture, banishment, and judgement. That mindset and environment is not a safe space for a teenager or a child to ask questions, be curious and discover who they truly are and what they believe.

The environment is not inclusive, it does not allow for anyone to see, debate and discuss all the different sides and experiences in life. And this is needed in development of one's self identity to solidify who they are and what they have a passion for, and what they believe. And they cannot achieve this autonomy because there is such an extreme judgment against anything different from the belief system and ideology in the group and home.

With all that harsh judgment, without being able to explore and have a safe space, and have discussions with a guide to provide wise counsel, then the empath emotionally is stunted. You don't know who you are, what you believe, or sometimes the real truth about how the World operates.

Bullying Affects Self Worth

Bullying is the use of force, coercion, hurtful teasing or threat, to abuse, aggressively dominate or intimidate. The behavior is often repeated and habitual. One essential prerequisite is the perception of an imbalance of physical or social power. - Wikipedia

An empath may have had a friend, sibling, parent or a classmate who continually bombarded them with negative words, and controlling them by diminishing their feelings, physically hurting them, or constantly pushing their boundaries and invading their privacy. And if one does not have that strong support system at home or with a teacher or therapist, they will learn to think this is normal, or are deserving of this maltreatment.

The constant toxic treatment chips away at their self esteem and it chips away at their spirit and confidence. Therefore bringing their self worth and identity lower and lower. Those negative words are powerful. And eventually they become their negative thoughts that turn inward toward themselves. The actions and words are like arrows, and they cause deep wounds at an early age that as an adult they have burried so far down inside that they are unaware of the emotional damage the abuser has inflicted on them. But there is hope, their actions and triggers are like small fissures, and cracks in the Earth. When they spew up the hot steam of anger and sadness these are signs there is a wound to face and heal.

That is again the point of this book to aid you in doing just that.

Conscious Parents Raise Strong Emotional Humans

"Just because our children came from us doesn't mean we get to dictate to them how it is they express their essence." - Dr. Shefali

The third way empaths are conditioned in toxic codependency is parental emotional neglect. This emotional paralysis is a big part of the parenting style of the patriarchy and many generations before us. The authoritarian parenting style of telling your child is antiquated and creates pain and strain on the relationship. And when we as the empathic child grow up and realize our identity was molded for us.

Let's clarify with some definitions again.

Authoritarian parenting is an extremely strict parenting style. It places high expectations on children with little responsiveness. As an authoritarian parent, you focus more on obedience, discipline, control rather than nurturing your child. - Web MD

Conscious parenting is a term used by various psychologists (and others) to describe a style of parenting that usually focuses more on the parent and how mindfulness can drive parenting choices.

It's rooted in a combination of Eastern-style philosophy and Western-style psychology. (In other words, a bringing together of meditation and self-reflection.)

Put most simply, conscious parenting asks that instead of striving to "fix" your child, parents look inward at themselves. Conscious parenting views children as independent beings (though admittedly still developing over time), who can teach parents to become more self-aware - Healthline.com

When we as children, teenagers, and adults are emotionally neglected, the lack of space held for all of our being is detrimental to our view of our selves.

Emotional neglect can be defined as a relationship pattern in which an individual's affectional needs are consistently disregarded, ignored, invalidated, or unappreciated by a significant other.

When the empath is ignored or banished for their big emotions that are filled with tears or anger, they feel they are to blame for the negative circumstances. This perpetual cycle, of unhappy feelings lead to feeling that stable parents love is removed leads them to people please and hiding those feelings. It also contributes to low self esteem and codependency by making sure that everyone else outside of them is happy. Making sure everyone outside of them gives you praise for your self worth. So that's why when the narcissist and the empath meet they hold onto that love bombing so tightly because they now take that on as their own self identity. The attention and adoration that is poured onto them is like a monsoon in a desert. And it feels so good because they've been parched and neglected for so long. But remember, as we will talk more in depth about in Chapter 5, the narcissist will remove that love just as fast. Leaving the empath with that, all too familiar, guilt feeling that negative circumstances are their fault. And they tolerate this emotional rollercoaster, because they are used to it. They don't know a healthy emotional pattern and the outside people's attention and praise is how they gauge their identity.

The good news is, no one has to be stuck in their five year old's emotional state. There is only one thing to do first, and that is face your shadows and hold space for them. Use the guided exercise to learn how to do this at the end of this chapter .

Amorous Curiosity

Life is an experience of learning and discovering through trial and error; that is a normal process. The toxic pattern of being reticent to talk about our bodies boldly and being scared and avoiding expressing what our body parts are for and what they are called is so antiquated. I believe we need to start talking to ourselves and the future generation about our body parts in a positive way. Without nicknames. As a mom I spoke to my children about the name of their body part, and that it is theirs only, and no one else can touch it, as early as three and a four years old. I think it's really important to have those conversations in a nonchalant, and composed manner. It's one of the many first ways to show them how to draw boundaries. I wish to have no weird feelings of guilt or shame of their bodies, the sexual organ as I did. I don't discuss at this young age the act of sex, but I've set the environment with talking about the birds and the bees of nature and animals in a scientific way, where they will feel comfortable to ask.

I don't subscribe to the concept that this topic must be hidden or a mystery or is a big off limits topic. If they can't feel safe to discuss it with me they may feel safe to discuss it with someone else and what if that person tells them about it in a negative tone? There are a lot of people that have been abused sexually by a family member or a friend of a family member, they then try to tell their mom and she doesn't believe them. This cycle must end. I think that's a really huge part of the Western history, suppressing and blocking out the ugly and not wanting to deal with it. But there's real abuse happening there's real trauma. There needs to be a safe conversation out in the open in homes. Because the more we keep it in the dark in the closet, the more that it will feed the ability to be hidden and for that darkness to continue to happen.

The next chapter I'll share another traumatizing event, and something else that happened unexpectedly to me in my life. This particular event really blacked out most of my childhood memories. It was a coping mechanism for my psyche to handle the trauma. I used to try to retrieve happy, joyful memories because when I looked back I only had a handful. I stopped trying because sometimes we must accept what is reality and be prepared to handle the truth that losing the memories is for the best.

Treasures Lost: Self Esteem

Main Human Design Element at play: *Open Will Center*

Learn more about Human Design in Chapter 12

A Gift from the Emotional Toolbox

If you have any experiences like this consentual yet guilt filled, or have had sexual abuse forced on you, reach out to a professional. They can help you heal through it and they can help you process it. Until we can get those blocks out of our body and the trauma released from the energy of our body we truly cannot move forward into living fully deeply, our true selves and heal.

In my situation, my bully was the first to come up to forgive and heal from during my marriage therapy twenty years after this occurred. When you bury it and do not heal the wound will affect your relationships.

Resources to find community and professionals: Tiaras, Tears & Triumphs, RAINN

Empath & Narcissist Podcast Season 1 Episode 7, Unleash Your Inner Warrior Sandy J {Tiaras, Tears & Triumphs} www.ravenscott.show/blog

Sexual assault hotline 800-656-HOPE (4673), www.victimconnected.org

Sexual abuse counselors directory www.betterhelp.com; Childhood sexual abuse help www.aamft.org, Joyful Heart Foundation, ASCA:Adult Survivors of Child Abuse, Male Survivor, Violence Unsilenced, Safe Horizon, Isurvive.

To dive deeper listen to Episode 58 The Forces that Drive Narcissism and How Unhealed Childhood Trauma Manifests on the Empath & Narcissist Podcast.

- GUIDED SHADOW WORK

What is the shadow? It sounds scary, but it truly is not.

The shadow is an archetype that consists of the sex and life instincts. The shadow exists as part of the unconscious mind and is composed of repressed ideas, weaknesses, desires, instincts, and shortcomings. The shadow forms out of our attempts to adapt to cultural norms and expectations.

Love is the core of our selves and Light. Love shines brightly dispelling the darkness. Full acceptance of one's self and full heart healing love dissolves all guilt, shame, and toxic subconscious patterns. It is here in this exercise we will safely face our repressed negative ideas of ourselves and heal while dispelling the darkness of the unconscious cycle.

"To be open to and inclusive of others, we must be fully open to and inclusive of ourselves." - Danielle La Porte

To begin, 1. Read this affirmation aloud.

"I trust in the wisdom within me to ground Divine energies onto the Earth. It is safe to be in my body. My divine perspective supports me in this illuminating work and supports my evolving ideas and revelations. May The Infinite deepen and expand my being to give and receive Love. I dissolve the fear, grievances, shame and guilt that is blocking my ability to live in full Love. I open my mind to be aware. I open my heart to be free. I open my wounds to love, heal and grow."

2. Now close your eyes and feel into your body by breathing deeply and slowly. Find the memories or thoughts that come up for you in your past as you read this chapter. When was the first time you felt this negative shame? What was the circumstance? How were you unsupported or abandoned? Sit with this for a few minutes. Allow the tears to well. Do not shove them down, do not stop them. Allow yourself to finally feel it all. And start to be the support your five year old self desires.

3. Now list all the wounds that come up. (ie: Fear of missing out, jealousy, selfishness, neediness, pain of abandonment, feeling desperate, unworthy, etc.)
The goal is to release all that separates ourselves from love and ultimate self inclusivity. To believe we deserve all love, abundance and healing we desire. This in turn will magnetize healthier relationships, higher vibration of pure peace and joy, and bounty. This ultimately fills up these deep core wounds and we minimize the triggers and pain points that we potentially could step on.

4. Now play the Gayatri Mantra in the Meditation Playlist on Raven Scott Show YouTube channel. And allow yourself to meditate on the glory of The Being who has produced this Universe; meditate that It enlighten your mind.

5. Now follow these journal prompts in honoring yourself.

What is so real that when I do it, it sources the rest of my life?

I am in awe and in wonder of myself! What do I admire about me?

What is one small change or shift that will create momentum toward who I want to be in this world?

3. VICTIMHOOD BLOCKS YOUR BEST LIFE

My legs are exhausted from climbing up and down the stairs. It's hot and sunny, in the quiet neighborhood where I grew up. My friend Heidi is helping me load all my belongings I've collected over my teenage years. My tiny Mini Cooper is filled to the brim with all my belongings with boxes of bathroom essentials, and clothes on hangers jammed up to the roof blocking the view in my rear window. I close all the doors and am ready to head off to my new apartment. I have a gut feeling of guilt and sadness. I am doing the thing to my parents I swore I wouldn't do and repeat the mistake my sister made. Is this how I move out of my parents? While they are away at work and not there to make me feel more guilty of my decision to avoid conflict. What a coward, I think. The terms I am moving out are under tense emotions. I am "making choices" my parents do not approve of. I look back one more time up at my bedroom window next to what was my sister's bedroom window. I wonder, "Is this how she left? With this feeling of avoiding disappointing them? Knowing this willbreak their hearts, but I just can't face them because I don't want to live by their rules anymore."

- **Desires and Betrayals**

You may be wondering, what happened to that bully Sally? I mentioned in the previous chapter that she had moved on to a different school after that year was finished. And then ironically the Universe brought me another opportunity to have resolution with her in the freshman year of High School. I made best friends with a girl, Jackie, a new student from Texas. And in her church she met another really great friend. One day she said, "Oh, you have to come and hang out and meet with my friend, she's so great." And I agreed to go with her. We pull up to the house and knock on the door and guess who opens the door! But Sally! This friend who turned into my bully four years passed without seeing and talking to her. I am now faced with her again. We were both shocked and cordial at the same time. We didn't say anything to our dear sweet Jackie, from Texas. And we carried on like we were brand new friends and all of that stuff in the past never happened. Which is a shame because that was such a great opportunity for us to have a one on one conversation about it and to hash it out but both of us were not taught how to do that and both of us were young and stupid. For a whole year we became the three musketeers. I think it's so strange and ironic at the same time. This person who wrecked my self esteem and tortured me at school is now in my life as a friend again. But it did give me surface closure to know we could be friends again. And for my inner child to know she wasn't a horrible enemy and she really was a kind person. Then our friend from Texas moved away and, obviously, we didn't stay connected. We then went our separate ways and carried on with our lives. It's a mystery to know where she is now, but I didn't need to know what her circumstances were to forgive her when I became an adult. During a relationship bootcamp in my thirties she was brought out of my shadows and into the light so I could exercise her from my closet. It is there I learned that you must pull the emotional wound out of the shadows into the light and make a big mess or have a big messy cry, and release that energy from your body in order to achieve full resolution before moving forward. If you do not, then the energy just stays stuck in your body and manifests as discomfort, patterns, or dis-ease. And she was truly healed and released from my psyche, I was no longer haunted by her again and I could truly nurture my self esteem.

- **The Person that Rocked my World.**

My sister and I are six years apart, she being my elder. I was like her baby. She helped my mom dress me, play with me, and she even interpreted my baby talk for my mother.

As we aged and she grew into herself and became a teenager, she did not waver from her strong willed spirit. Everyone in my family is strong willed or stubborn. They clung to their strict Catholic rules because they feared the same pattern would occur from their past. It was strongly stressed there was to be no sex before marriage. Period.

I don't know about you, but I find that can be tricky as a teenager. Your hormones are running, the pleasure factor is impossible to stop. Speaking from experience now, I have the theory that you should try on the bicycle before. And talk about safety, prevention, and advocate for "consent and condoms."

I also understand that when you do have intimacy with someone your souls link, so you have to be picky. Before you try on the bike that you really should test him out that he truly values you and loves you.

But I digress. Back the story. When I was eleven, and she was seventeen she had a boyfriend she really loved. They became pregnant while she was still in High School and living at home. What a way to grow up fast!

She has always wanted to be a mom since she was a little girl.

There was no question about keeping it or not. One day she came to me during my school hours and pulled me out of class, into the hallway, to tell me she was moving out and that she "loved me." She moved out the same time, during the work day, that I did years later. She didn't want tears, conflict or heartbreak. We both moved out in the same exact way. We knew their beliefs and since they didn't agree we felt that left us with the only choice to "do it on our own."

I am grateful she didn't want to abandon me without saying goodbye. But for me at eleven it was still traumatic. I started crying immediately. I hugged her and bawled my eyes out, and went back into class, trying to suck it up, and was in a haze the rest of the day. I didn't know she was pregnant, I didn't know why she left, she just left. And I did feel abandoned and in shock.

My teacher was such an angel to me. The rest of the school year she always was extra careful and paid attention to my emotions. I really wasn't the same that whole school year after that day.

I visited her a handful of times throughout my childhood, when her family moved to the East Coast for her husband's career I visited only twice. I did not communicate with her on a regular basis as cell phones were not readily available yet and she was busy with her new baby. When we reconnected in my thirties, it was like meeting a new friend and starting from square one.

- **The victim**

When I try to retrieve memories in my childhood many are blacked out. They don't exist. I have a handful but a lot of them are not there in my memory bank. I believe that was due to the trauma. Due to divine intervention and hard work, my sister and I now, as adults, have a relationship that is on the mend, yet tumultuous. She has shared memories and I discover a whole new event that I didn't remember. The joining of our young children together in social bonding has really been a blessing to be able to have that healing happen. Life is not perfect and we both have a lot to learn in relating to each other. But we go through life to learn lessons through experiences.

I believe life happens *for* you not *to* you. That is the state of mind that I'm writing this book.

I was not able to move forward, forgive and feel clarity until I stopped holding on to the idea that she abandoned me. She was just trying to live her life, and I was just caught in the wake of that. I was stuck in that pattern of thinking she did not care about me. And while she may have cared for me, she placed herself first. And everything she didn't do that I expected a sister to do triggered me. And it still triggered me into my adulthood until I accepted the truth she was incapable of loving how I deserved. In the lows of our relationship I learned to draw upon the joy of my family, I have created, to heal and move on. I adapted and instead of the family whom I was born into being my anchor, I released her and found inner strength to be my grounding. Siblings are not always your safe person; it's sad, but true. And blood is not thicker than water. Trust is earned. Relationships take effort. And since she has showed me time and again that she lacks the tools to love me, I let go of the expectations of my ideal, fantasy relationship with her. Her challenge is she abhors conflict and desires bliss, but is stuck with not having the emotional tools to be able to attain harmony.

The phrase "you are welcome anytime" that she repeated to me was the covert self absorbtion of lack of responsibility for nurturing our relationship through communication, compromise, and empathy while gaslighting me with an open invitation. This was my harsh truth I had to accept. And as many hours as I invested in driving to her house, she lacked reciprocating with the same energetic effort while excluding me from plans that involved my parents. This is another lesson in independence and no longer being codependent. As I do have legitimate reasons to feel like the victim I found that I needed to work to stop accepting the role of the victim. This is real mental and spiritual work that we are all capable of. And you may feel if you let go you are allowing the offender to get away with it. However, holding onto the poisonous feelings of hate, unforgiveness, bitterness and pain only hurts you and Karma will come back in retribution for you. It's not your job to punish them. Now that I have let go I can experience life in a freer, more joy filled way. We can have heartfelt conversations that bring healing, laughter and tears. We live life fully, not numbing the pain and going through the motions making sure not to step on the elephant we have shoved under the rug.

We all have in our subconscious and with ancestral line patterns that are beyond our recognition and understanding, and we're all trying to do our best to make amends in our relationships moving forward. And realizing we both repeated the same pattern made it even more apparent there was a force more powerful that we could comprehend that influenced our decisions. Culture, religion, authoritarian rule and the complex energies of the human desires led us to be independent and make our own self sovereign rules. You may question this with a belief that without religion and rules that govern everyone there isn't order and protection. And God has these rules through love. And I would ask, did God say you should blindly follow an oppressive ideology over common sense in relating to your child and being their teacher? That to me is nonsensical controlling behavior rather than a guide for your child.

It's important for us not to enable our children to be the victim. When something bad might happen we want to give them consolation and be a safe place, but we also want them to know and understand that this is just part of life and bad things are going to happen and not everything is going to be perfect. Show empathy, teach them vulnerability, and the power of choices. This is what we lacked in our early child development. But we can now be our inner child's parent and show ourselves the same compassion and wisdom to grow our emotional intelligence. So what can we do ourselves that we can control? Sometimes all we can do is have the mindset that we are learning through struggle; even when the lesson is unclear. And in order to grow and mature it is important to not give up and apply discipline to our self improvement. Creating daily practices that nurture expansion. So that when a struggle shows up we are stronger and equipped to handle it. And it gives us empathy for the other people going through similar struggles.

True belonging is including and belonging to ourselves first. Self sacrifice is not a virtue, it is detrimental.

> *"The acceptance we bring to ourselves helps us stop relying solely on others for validation. If we outsource our validation to other people we are just going to be doggy paddling in a whirlpool."* - Sarah Faith Gottessdeiner. Moonbeaming podcast (June 16 2022 episode)

If you want to see your vast potential, you must drop your defensiveness equally as you draw powerful boundaries. If we are not making a conscious decision to transform and break the toxic patterns, then our brain automatically operates in conditioned subconscious patterns.

Treasure lost: A sister

Main Human Design Element at play: Defined Ajna - My mind conceptualizes consistently and gets fixed on ideas. It can be the cause of judgement, blaming, and a fixed mindset on the lower frequency rather than a gracious, gentle, growth mindset. I locked onto the idea that she abandoned me, rather than accepting that her actions don't define me or directly relate to my self confidence and her love for me.

Dive deeper into this topic in S3 episode 52. Taking control of your life from the Narcissist.

-   EMOTIONAL RELEASE PAINTING EXERCISE:

Emotional releasing through painting is one of my favorite ways to transform the internal narrative.

The first step is to gather your materials.

1. 2 Canvas or thick paper any size 6" x 9" is my favorite size
2. Paints of any sort : acrylic, or water paint
3. Paint brushes - nothing fancy
4. Cup of water and paper towels

Then set yourself up on a table. Here you will close your eyes and imagine the colors that you see or feel that represent your feelings. You may be feeling mad, sad, bitter, etc. Pick those colors out and paint the canvas in those colors. Don't worry about what form or shapes to paint, allow yourself to freely brush strokes you feel. They could be big and swishy, or they could be sharp dots or strokes. This is your body's way to get the energy out however it needs. If you run out of white space, perfect! Keep painting over other colors and fully express your feelings on your canvas.

Once you are fully finished and can't paint anymore strokes of your feelings. Put that aside. Take three very slow and deep breaths in and out. Count to four in and count to four out; eyes closed preferably.

Next take your second blank canvas out and now close your eyes again. Envision yourself free of this thought. How do you feel without the thoughts of the negative narrative? How do you act? Who are you without these feelings? Envision or feel the colors that you feel as this new person. Now paint them on your second canvas. Same abstract concept as the first canvas. No shapes, shapes if you want, strokes of any variation and feeling. Fill up the canvas and fully express your feelings until you run out of creativity.

Now put your supplies down and view your canvases side by side. Evaluate your creations and see how you can control your outcome of your creations. The same is true of your mind and state of being. Which canvas do you prefer? Your thoughts are powerful and so is the story in your head. To feel better and grow it takes releasing the negative and fully sharing it, then transforming it to "Who would I be and how would I feel if I didn't have this negative thought?" This doesn't invalidate the thought, but it does put it into perspective and gives you control over your internal narrative. You get to choose which canvas you want to keep and live out.

4. FROM A NARCISSIST MAGNET

to a Narcissist Repellant

Sitting on the edge of my bed, all I remember from last night was partying in the elevator after drinking two bottles of Mike's Hard Lemonade with Everclear added in while it was very late and not a soul awake. I looked down at my feet with the light shining way too bright in my eyes. It sounded thrilling in the moment, but now that I am sober it wasn't that fantastic after all.

How did I get lost? How did I let myself and my treasures get buried under the other person's talents? All through my twenties I looked for myself in all the wrong places and outside of my being. I felt overly confident all at the same time of feeling lost and constantly confused. I discarded and buried my amazing treasures for love, approval and the idea of growing up. Why did I think those treasures within me were trash? And why did I let so many relationships go and let my current love affair smother my light?

The answers lie within my centers and gates in my Human Design Chart. When we live out of alignment with our soul we transfer our motives and experience pain and frustration.

My motivation as a human is hope, and when I am out of alignment and do not see hope in sight, my transference is guilt. I allow guilt to drive all my decisions and please the other person. I always felt a need for control to prove my worthiness. I constantly felt alone and a foreigner even in the midst of my classmates. But I found peace in always searching for God at that time and was most at home in nature and outside with my horse.

The answer also lies in a deep lack of trust in my spiritual foundation due to the hedge of Catholicism, manipulation and lack of information I was given about how the world even exists according to science versus according to an ancient text. After learning about evolution at the age of eighteen, my whole world was shaken. I was lied to, I felt betrayed, and angry at the God of my childhood. I searched outside myself and tried and experimented to find my own way in the world without my parents and their foundation. The problem was my new "savior" was more lost than I could recognize. We became codependent on each other in a very unhealthy way. And I grew comfortable in my cage of this toxic relationship. I have the gate (trait) of fear of the future in my Spleen Center defined. You may check on your chart if you have it, it's #57. If you need help just reach out to me, the information is in depth in Chapter 12.

- **The Awkward Granola Girl**

After my sister left I invested a lot of time at my aunt's house every weekend. She had two daughters older than me. And on the weekends I was the third sibling. I cherish those moments and enjoyed the adventures and fun times that I experienced. My sister cousins and I would dress up for Halloween and trick or treat, swim at the local lake, and do crafts.

After my traumatic friend experience I would only make one friend each year and it was always the new student. Without being conscious of this nuance, I realize now I didn't trust the students, due to them all turning against me that year. And it makes sense now upon discovering my Human Design, being a 6/2 role model / hermit, I always was selected as the leader role in charge of things. It was a Cathlic School, so I stepped into the role of choir leader, and at church I led a breakout group of 50 other students with another adult leader. So my leadership roles came out of my natural leadership qualities of being a 6 line role model. I felt so much responsibility all the time; even my hobby of horse riding and ownership I felt responsible every day to exercise and let him get out of his "cage." And every event or moment I was the one to step in and take charge. The hermit part was my love for nature and my inclination to keep to myself. On top of the trauma, it just forced me more to be a hermit and hide out and get through school. I was socially awkward due to this combination because I wasn't cool, or fun, or even acting my appropriate age. My peers didn't know how to relate to me and I to them.

- **Teenage crush**

When it came to boys I also felt a strong responsibility to not repeat the mistake my sister made and I stayed busy with school, cheerleading, choir, worship team at school, and worship team at church, and leading the group at church, and riding and taking care of my horse- oh ya and homework. I left no time for boys. Even when there was that off occasion a boy would flirt with me and want to snuggle, but that's as far as I wanted it to go. I carried the burden of being a good girl, I wanted to do the right thing and I wanted to be a role model as a Catholic. I was so guarded, and put up the aura of don't get too close or make a move. And at the same time I was devastated, and based my self worth on whether the boys liked me or not because I was still playing that ugly dog loop over and over in my head.

I was primed to be a victim for a strong willed, overbearing, narcissist to brainwash me into loving him. I also have to point out that in my Human Design chart my solar plexus is open; that made me a people pleaser, and my will center is open and it amplifies other people's ideas to take over my own will. With gate 50 in my defined Spleen center, I have a fear of failing to take care of loved ones & responsibilities. Those two centers being open with the combination of my social awkward childhood are what I believe made me prey to this toxic scenario. Do you have those in your chart? And do you experience those same codependent tendencies?

- **The Acacians**

Senior year of high school our youth group grew so big we couldn't fit into the local mountain summer camp campus. So they created their own camp that fit the whole youth group over four weeks of the summer. They found a property with a barn that had two loft spaces and an actual bathroom for the pastor and volunteers. There was a lake, a dirt trail through the Pine Tree forest, a field with horses, and an abandoned house. I actually took care and bandaged one of the horses with my horse owning skills and knowledge who was cut on a barbed wire fence.

I was on the worship team and sang every week, so naturally as a Line 6 role model I was asked to go and I gladly accepted. I spent the whole month there with my friends and fellow bandmates, the youth pastor, and other volunteers that I adored. It's one of my fondest memories of my childhood.

Four of us volunteers thrived in nature. We slept in tents in a meadow below the barn with a supervisor in an RV to protect us from bears. We called ourselves The Acacians.

This also is the place where I got to know a fellow bandmate through conversation. He was really tall, handsome, and charming. He was the boy who was out of my reach, so to speak, a boy whose family had status in the church, and appeared so wealthy and regal; plus he fit the physical description of a Disney movie prince. His name was Lance.

Every night after all the campers would go to sleep five of us friends, including Lance, would sit on the porch of the barn, and we would look up at the stars, and he would talk about the stars and he would talk about everything. He just was a talker, (he had an open throat center) and he had so much wealth of knowledge as I learned, after we became romantic, that he read encyclopedia books as a young child. I was so drawn to his wealth of knowledge. He would talk and then I would fall asleep to his narration. This should have been his first red flag because this wouldn't be the first time this pattern would appear in our relationship. And my first red flag should have been that he didn't really ask a lot of questions about me.

What is it about your first love, that you let go of all their flaws and focus on their strengths? When you do that you miss the red flags. He had a calming energy with his self confidence, and I felt so comfortable and attracted to him in a non butterfly way. The feeling was very neutral and in the beginning of our friendship he sought a romantic relationship with one of the other Acacians. We spent time as friends for months after that summer camp trip. He liked the feeling of me worshipping him, but this is what created this unhealthy pattern.

- **Fireworks**

As we developed our friendship, we spent many hours after church spending time together one on one. I was always available and reliable, and he was also. We enjoyed each other's company and one night he surprised me with a kiss. I really wasn't expecting it. I was opening my door to his car on the passenger side to exit, and he called "Ray." I turned around and he leaned in for the kiss. I kissed him back. And it made my stomach all a flutter, I felt like I was walking on a people mover all the way to my parents' front door. And the electricity in my body felt like fireworks went off! I closed the front door and leaned against the inside of it catching my breath and pinching myself. *Did he really like me? Did he just kiss me?!* I thought. I felt ecstatic....My father drowsily called out, "Hey Ray" I gathered myself up and unsuccessfully called out calmly "Hey Dad."

The explosion of chemistry and my desperation for a boy to be physically interested in my "ugly self" clouded my judgment and I didn't care if he was right for me or not. Of course on the surface and if written on a business card he was right for me.

"Handsome Tall Male

Member of same church and religion

Smart, funny, beautiful mother & grandmother. Kind family.

Available for a relationship with a smart pretty girl."

"Hired!" He fit all the boxes I was conditioned to accept in a boyfriend.

He made the world look beautiful and relieved me of my constant weight of responsibility. We enjoyed breakfast for dinner, midnight drives, music, fine dining, Posh lifestyle, concerts, and staycations. It was a blast. We laughed, made love, danced to music. What else could a new romance ask for? The ocean was both our favorite places to relax. Hanging with our friend group was all part of our normal routine on Wednesdays after church.

I had never been shown I was pretty, objectified and desired for my body and I craved that attention to finally prove I was worthy and loved. I put myself out there like a high end street walker, except for an audience of one. However, I didn't mind the heads I turned along the way. It made me feel amazing, arrived and high up in status. I had a handsome man on my arm, and he had a beautiful woman on his. I held my head high, I strutted around in my stilettos believing I was better than most everyone. I hopped in the convertible feeling like I was the bomb. I showed all of my classmates that I was something and not the weird girl who was nothing. Outwardly I proved to them I had arrived and they were still in the same struggling spots. I had overcome my childhood past and grown into a successful working wealthy twenty something year old. It felt good and I glowed with extra confidence and sex appeal. I put my self worth in the reactions and beliefs that others thought I was hot and successful as well and I hustled at work, gained a managerial position in corporate in my twenties and partied until I dropped- literally.

I was 110% all in. This is my tendency when I am committed to a circumstance or person. I can't help it. But if I had more self esteem, I would have approached it much more casually. *Sure I will date him for a bit and weigh my options.* Should have been my thoughts. He was after all my first boyfriend as a young adult. But I was too conditioned to believe this was the only chance, he was all I had and I had arrived. Where else would I go from here?

This would have been the conversation with my Spirit Guide/ or any sane person had I asked about it, and if I had connected back then.

- Spirit Guide   "Ray Did he ask you about your desires? Like get to know you?"
- Me   "No"
- Spirit Guide   "Any questions about what your dreams are?"
- Me   "No"
- Spirit Guide   "If you want children?"
- ME   "No"
- Spirit Guide "Then how do you think HE is the one to commit your soul to? Run girl! Run!"

I didn't trust anyone. I didn't even trust my mom to decide who was right for me, based on a previous experience that denied a beautiful mocha skinned boy a relationship with me because the advice I received was "The Bible says to not be unequally yoked." Not until after I regurgitated those words, and his heart was broken, did I realize at fourteen that that was racist. *Never again,* I swore to myself would I trust anyone else to decide for me. It hurt me as deeply as it hurt him to have spoken those words and having any ounce of dislike for others' differences. I know in my soul we are all one humankind and our desires and insides are all the same. In that circumstance it was my fear of making a mistake and being a responsible good daughter.

So I trusted only me, myself , I, from that moment on. I wanted to belong and rise above all those who taunted me in my childhood. I wanted recognition and admiration that I was pretty and desirable. If I had the previous conversation with myself or Spirit Guides, I believe our relationship wouldn't have gone so far. He made it very clear he didn't want it to be serious. In my desperation to be loved and to please I agreed, knowing that would change in the future. I just wished it wouldn't. I latched on like a crazy girl in the movies. After I harrowingly moved out of my parent's house, I had my own place, but I spent all my time at his place, so I moved in with him. Then he made it very clear there would be no marriage or children in the future. I ignored it as immaturity and I wasn't ready either. But then as time went on I was emotionally in too deep to give up and I literally feared the future and thought no one ever was going to love me other than him. And he eventually made sure he enforced that lie in my head.

- **Worthy**

To all you empaths out there chasing fake love, this is for you. I feel your anguish. The trick in breaking that painful cycle, with a love, a sibling, or a parent is to stop chasing and start fostering love for your own self. Relationships are a two way street. A game of tennis. If you find you are always serving and "the ball" (effort) is not being hit back over the net, then you are currently investing in a one sided relationship.

> *What is meant for you will be. The people that want to be in your life will show up and be present. You don't need to convince, manipulate, or figure out how to have someone*

present. If this resonates and you feel a slight ache in your gut as you read this, you have experienced this unpleasant interaction.

You are worthy of true love, worthy of light, worthy of truth, worthy of joy, worthy of laughter in the bedroom, worthy of delight and worthy of living your truest self's purpose. Start searching and looking within yourself to find your treasures within yourself designed by the Divine to bless other people in this world.

And those who aim to bring you down are already below you.

Treasure lost: My innocence

Main Human Design Element at play: Open Will center. When this is open you are more prone to amplify other's desires. You don't even realize it because you adopt it as your own. You truly need to strengthen your inner authority to make decisions that are aligned with yourself, and not get sucked into another's desires. Read more about Human Design in Chapter 12.

Dive deeper into this topic in S3 Episode 64 What is Projection and How Narcissists use it to Manipulate with Dr. Marni Hill, on the Empath & Narcissist Podcast.

- INNER CHILD MEDITATION

Do this to heal any trauma, pain, or expectations imposed on you at a very young age. This clears out the negative energy, releases you from their expectations and pain. This energy gets passed down from one generation to another. This is a way to remove those burdens and break the chords of the past.

If I had done this before meeting Lance, I truly believe I would have had the self confidence and respect to break it off with him within the first six months. I would have kept my apartment, continued on in my life with confidence and attracted the right partner that loved, respected and cherished me. However, I also accept we all have a unique Karmic path and this is just part of my journey.

I highly recommend doing the most single, powerful meditation to heal past wounds and trauma. When you do you will transform and heal the brokenness inside you that allows you to put up with circumstances and people that do not serve you. You will be able to hold space and love the most difficult people with boundaries. You will be able to love and care for yourself and with your cup full your love will overflow for those around you.

This is a practice I recommend doing every day for twenty eight days straight. If that is not feasible, once a week will work, just not as quickly. It is imperative you take time to do this meditation so you may be free from the burdens, expectations, and negative patterns in your life. Fifteen minutes is all it takes.

This will be the most transforming, and healing exercise you will do for yourself in this journey. And that's either going to heal your relationship you're in because you're going to come from a place of health, or it's going to tell you exactly what your next step is to be and that might be leaving that relationship.

Some instances your inner child has been locked away and hidden in a dungeon for so long they are initially unresponsive to your interaction. They are hurt, angry, untrusting of your efforts to hold and play with them due to your many years of neglect. It is not your fault, we all are conditioned to lock our child up as we grow older. It may take time to gain your inner child's trust. In doing the exercise below your inner child may not want to sit next to you, sit in your lap, or touch you. That is ok, allow them the freedom to experience learning how to trust you first and over time with continual growth of your relationship they will come to love, trust and embrace you. Which is you truly embracing yourself.

When you experience spells of emotional uncontrol, you are encountering your inner child screaming out for attention. To you on the outside it may appear as a pattern you are dying to fix and stop feeling sadness or pain in this emotional area. Just recently after doing many years of work on myself and thinking I had healed my inner child, she brought to light a deep sadness and wound of abandonment I thought was finalized. A family member visited my home and in that short visit I felt and observed myself feeling anxious about anticipating their leaving. I wasn't able to enjoy the moment, and when they left, I felt a deep emotional shock wave of sadness. It brought my thoughts spiraling into I am lonely, I am abandoned, I am disconnected from everyone. Where in reality these were emotions of my inner child from long ago when my sister left and moved out of the house.

I immediately knew I needed to tend and care for my inner child. I spent time meditating, journaling, soaking in a bath, however

I could not shake the feeling of sadness. It was a deep wave of energy that needed to be felt all the way through and come out of me.

Tosha Silver says "Tears are the ice melting in our hearts."

And if I continued to press it down and lock it up to "heal" it, that would only do myself emotional damage and keep a dark energy orb in my body. Of course my partner knew not what to do and left me alone, only because when I have felt this in the past I would lash out and blame him for my sadness. The inner child holds back on no one. However this in turn reinforces the inner child's narrative that I am truly alone. And only I can hold and console her to let her know I am taking care of her and she is not alone.

Sometimes tending to your inner child is not a one time and then done event. It is a true relationship and you must treat it as such. I listened to a book by Tosha Silver and in it she spoke of an expert who's favorite line was " There is always something." These spells and triggers are going to happen, it is the cycle of karma and the process of evolving as a person. It is how we react in these moments that define if we are evolved and open to taking in the lesson our inner child and the Universe has in store for us. There is no holy land of arrival that we experience no emotions or suffering in this life such as nirvana describes. This life is for us to constantly be in the lesson battlefield and emotions are the direct conduit for our behaviors, ideas, and spiritual enlightenment to evolve.

In conclusion, this Inner Child is never ending and recognizing the child is a lifelong journey. Sometimes the Divine brings us circumstances and triggers to draw out the shadow and heal the pain buried deep within. A supercharged intervention from the Divine. So take heed of your emotions and recognize and acknowledge them. Embrace them as you would a guest, experience what they bring up, and then release them as they leave spreading clarity breadcrumbs in their wake.

I was told by a friend and psychologist, Jena Jake, to carry around a scarf or a pillow on your body, as a symbol of your inner child. Having the reminder of her around your neck will help remind you that you are beautiful, you are precious, and you are loved. You, as an adult *CAN* take care of yourself and inner child in many ways daily through:

1. Read an affirmation
2. Call a friend
3. Dine on a special treat
4. End a habit that is not serving you
5. Find the fun in life: Do something out of the ordinary
6. Go for a walk in nature
7. Exercise, get your blood pumping
8. Sleep in
9. Inhale aromatherapy
10. Ask for help
11. Balance fun and work
12. Set boundaries
13. Say No
14. Light a candle
15. Celebrate you accomplishments
16. Color or draw
17. Bubble Bath
18. Journal
19. Buy yourself flowers
20. Drink a glass of a special mocktail
21. Read a book
22. Buy something special for yourself
23. Empath Protection Meditation
24. Writing a forgiveness letter
25. Playing outside
26. Reading
27. Dancing
28. Yoga / Stretch

29. Have a good cry
30. Organizing or cleaning a closet
31. Inner Child Meditation
32. Wear a scarf to signify your inner child

Look inside yourself and love yourself again. The single most powerful exercise you can do to heal yourself, is *inner child work*. This guided meditation is a start and will release all of the conditioning, fears, burdens, expectations of your parents placed on you as a seven year old child. You will discover magic, joy, and healing powers in this meditation.

Watch & Practice the Free Inner Child meditation at Raven Scott Show YouTube channel. You can access the whole library in the Meditation Playlist.

Here is the transcript:

Find a comfortable place to sit or lie down in a quiet space that is private. Close your eyes. Elongate your spine nice, tall or long. Take a deep breath in and a deep breathe out. Place your left hand on your heart and your right hand on your belly. Take a deep breath in again and feel the rise of your belly and chest and out through mouth, ha. Take a deep in and out. Ha. ...Now breathe nice and easy now and steady. Relaxed breathing.

And find yourself in a white blank room. And in this room, you start to hear the sound and see the items of your childhood. Come into existence in your mind in this and you see the wall paper, your bed, your bedding. You feel the sheets, you smell the homemade smells, you hear toys, laughter and any common noises that occurred in your childhood home. You are now in your childhood home at age 5 or 7. You imagine yourself wandering out of the bedroom and into your living room.

Imagine yourself standing in your childhood living room.

Now see each parent standing in front of you. Or the guardians that took care of you. And one at a time they take turns and come to you with their fears and expectations. Each individual fear and expectation is a brick . They pile them into your hands in the form of bricks. You feel them piling higher and higher above your head. Hear or feel the fears and expectations expressed of each brick that is placed in your hands. You feel them getting heavy and they each carry more and more weight you have to hold. Your arms are shaking. They finish placing the bricks and they are too much for you to bear. Just as you think you are going to drop them, see your adult self walk into the room.

Then your adult self enters. And you remove the bricks from your child self's hands and place them on the floor. You take your inner child by the hands, look them in the eye and tell them, "those burdens do not belong to you. You do not need to stay here anymore. You are free to leave. Come with me." You coax yourself out of the room holding hands "come with me"

You both exit the front door and you lead your child self out of the house and living room, and everything disappears behind you. You walk down a dirt path and approach a large iron gate adorned with gold scrolls and climbing vines. As an adult, while still holding your child self's hand, you push open the gate. There are many stairs in front of you looking downward. There is a staircase where you start to descend together into a beautiful garden.

You climb down, down, down, you climb… Down, down, down. You arrive in this garden at the bottom of the staircase. You release hands because you feel safe. You feel at peace, and mesmerized by the beauty. You start on a winding path along a river and you smell the Jasmine, and Gardenia flowers, you see trees lining the path blocking you from the sun, rose bushes, and short ground covering moss. The violets and petunias, you hear the birds singing, feeling the hummingbirds buzzing, and see the daffodils standing proud. Soak it in.

Let your inner child roam free and play, laugh and discover the garden. You observe them. They may want to run, do cartwheels, skip and twirl in this beautiful space. They may pick a flower, or just smell the sweet gardenias. You hear the trickling river, feel the gentle breeze and you hear the swaying leaves in the tree's branches. Observe.

You may encounter butterflies, which symbolize Spirit Guides. Or you may stop and visit with a fairy, if you do so, soak up their magical healing powers.

You notice there is a pink and gold pixie dust that poofs off of the garden's contents when bumped or touched.

You now join hands together and walk a little further down the path. Each step and movement you see the trail of gold and pink dust. You reach a grass clearing near the river and see the gold and pink pixie dust now raining down constantly. It's swirling in the gentle breeze and fairies flying by swishing a new trail fresh over your head. You see it fall onto your head and feel it itch your nose. Let your inner child explore and do as you feel needed in this grass clearing.

You smile and delight your child's freedom and joy in this space. Then you spot a Willow Tree and make your way together over to sit under it. You invite your inner child to sit with you. Ask your inner child, "What do you need to tell me?" Pause, wait, and listen. This may be audible, this may be a feeling, or it may be a group of words, or a color. Note what your inner child tells you.

Then you ask your inner child, "What do you want or need?" Pause, wait, and listen. Again this may come in a form that only you understand. Note what your inner child tells you.

Then you invite your inner child to sit in your lap. Place your right hand over your inner child's heart 12" away from your chest. You will now take seven OM's to heal with the Om vibration and transmute your inner child into yourself. On the fourth OM you will start to imagine your child melding into your body and your hand moves closer until it touches your chest.

Take a deep breath in and OM on your exhale. 4x

Take a deep breath in and OM on your exhale 3 x fusing your child into your body.

Breathe normally and calmly, keep your eyes closed.

Soak up the peaceful healing of this garden for another breath or two. Remain present in this space.

Ask your Spirit Guides, Guardian Angels, and Fairies to freely remain with you or leave as they choose. Thank your inner child for the advice and promise that you will tend to their needs.

Slowly wiggle, your fingers and toes, and blink your eyes open, finding yourself back in your Earth plane body.

Thank yourself for the time well invested in your spiritual and emotional well being. Namaste

5. LOVEBOMBING & DEVALUATION

The Narcissists Arsenal

I t's cold and raining and I'm pounding on the glass door. He's locked me outside in my lingerie! Really?! With the balcony on a cliff and no exit route in sight, I am stuck to keep knocking and begging to be let inside. I give up, shiver out in the cold, and pray for him to open it soon. By the way, I had quit praying to "God" years before this moment. I don't know how this happened, what I did wrong. We started arguing over who knew what, then I was pushed out the door. It was mind boggling, just a few hours ago he was rubbing my feet and laughing.

- **Codependency**

"1. the state of being mutually reliant, for example, a relationship between two individuals who are emotionally dependent on one another.

2. a dysfunctional relationship pattern in which an individual is psychologically dependent on (or controlled

by) a person who has a pathological addiction (e.g., alcohol, gambling). —codependent *adj.*"

American Psychological Association

-   **Duel with the Devil**

For the first three years of Lance and I's romance we had fun, I had no idea that I was slowly being groomed to be in a committed emotionally abusive relationship.

When we first met I, by no means, was a party girl. I was a good girl, remember. A worship leader, a youth group leader, chaplain. I was the goody two shoes perfect, you know, granola girl. I was very happy. I was very pleased with my life of service. I also was tired of the responsibility at the same time. I wore no makeup confidently. Because I felt betrayed by the withholding of information and sheltering from science, my love and attraction deepened with Lance sharing this with me. He opened my eyes to a whole new world. It was a perfect set up for him to have power over me. I placed him on a pedestal, he was my new "Savior".

As I rebelled and let go of all my responsibilities, I did have a lot of fun partying. I mentally threw all my responsibilities and cares to the wind. I was able to become this woman as an alternate ego and feeling free from the burden of responsibility felt like I was finally alive. I dressed up, did my hair and makeup like a model in the magazines and I took pleasure in people not recognizing me. The pressure put upon me after my sister left, and my own self, and energy of my Profile type line six in my human design chart, put too much pressure to make good choices and be good. And when I reached the breaking point at age eighteen it exploded back in my face. I said "Screw it! Let's have fun!" I drank as much alcohol as I possibly could. I partied, went out to clubs, danced with girlfriends in seductive ways, tried to pick fights with big bouncers, and pushed the limits. I was up for anything and was making up for the fun that I missed out on. That was great for a time, but then that was not in alignment with who I was. I found myself in a perpetual deeper vortex of trying to out fun myself and my partner egged that on. Lance had a propensity for excitement and hated the mundane. Every night was a new night to do "it" funner, looser, longer, yet in his same controlled environment. He was a creature of habit and ate the same food at the same restaurant and the experiences, try as I may to make them exciting, they were boring and mundane while under the disguise of fun and flamboyant. The only times I truly had a blast partying was when I went out with friends without Lance. He always had to control the scenario and it had to be posh and elegant.

I had a successful sales job, I made good money and drove a luxury car all before 30. I was superficially happy with my status and all of these exterior things. But my life was a roller coaster. On the outside looking in you could tell I was not satisfied or fulfilled. My friends at work noticed and gently tried to help me free myself of this abusive relationship. I would come to work every Saturday hung-over, pale, and heart broken.

- **Narcissistic Abuse**

Lance & I's relationship grew to be mutually reliant; we were the comfort zone for each other. I was up for anything and tried anything once, especially in the bedroom. We had extravagant dates at the same sophisticated four or five star restaurants and I felt elevated in status, but the lifestyle was wearing on me. Life started to feel mundane and like work in every aspect. One can only eat at the same restaurant so many times, and drive the same route, and have the same routine every day. It was work to make money, work to sell my "fun Raven" personality, work to please, and work in the bedroom. The only area he craved variety was in regards to our sex life. He desired more and longer, and hotter in the bedroom. It evolved from fun to a dysfunctional relationship pattern where he controlled my actions to feed his pathological sex and alcohol addiction.

He was obsessed with it being more and more like pornographic videos on steroids. He would convince me it was hotter to watch porn and then have it playing while we did it. He then in turn convinced me while I was intoxicated to shoot our own pornographic footage. That footage is still alive and in existence today and has been used to black mail me already. The threats were that our activities were consensual, however when alcohol and codependency are in effect the consent is not sound and are null and void.

Alcohol was the substance involved in every romantic night, and he was convinced it would "loosen me up." It sure did and then I would pass out before he could accomplish all he imagined. Which then resulted in him getting mad and not speaking to me the next day. I didn't always pass out, sometimes he was just bored and we had plenty of fights while I was awake. His perpetual insults when I was at my most vulnerable were cruel and I would lash out. I remember screaming back and forth at each other, and throwing things. That was both our open solar plexus (emotional) centers amplifying each other by the way.

Then the next day we would make up, have a conversation on how *I* needed to fix things and all would be right. He would dote on me, rub my feet, and even buy me flowers to ensure I felt loved again. The love and affection in conjunction to his "all-knowing" solutions to our problems was how he controlled me to accept this vicious emotional abuse.

But sure enough he would fall into the pattern of being disappointed and he would put me down once more, become disgusted and silent toward me. I would get tired of waiting for him to consummate after four hours, and as patient as I was, he would give up. He then would project his insecurities onto me, hurling insults at me with his words. I would take the responsibility on myself that I wasn't hot enough, or doing the right move to help him get off. I internalized it as my fault and I constantly was in pleasing mode. It was exhausting because he could never be content. He even went so far to buy pills on the black market that mimicked Viagra and he convinced me, this would be the answer this time.

While on this rollercoaster I became isolated from my family. I listened and trusted him and I felt so much pain from my parents judgement, and condemnation of my sinful choices that pleasing this new master of emotional tyranny seemed better than facing my mistakes.

We both had hermit lines so we held each other closer and stopped talking to those who disagreed with him or made us feel judged. There were many years I did not call or go home for Christmas. Our leaning on each other and my embracing his family gave him more control over my social situation and I sought his counsel for everything.

My low self esteem and his feeding the lies that I was dumb and ignorant made me lean on his advice even more. I just couldn't handle the emotional turbulence of his pushing me away and pulling me close. But I was strong and I was a fighter. And I fought for seven years for stability in our relationship.

The terrifying idea of what was out there in the dark abyss of the future prohibited me from believing that there was someone else better for me. And put me in a desperate situation that lasted for seven years. I made seven attempts to move out and leave, and all seven times I missed him and felt lost without his influence and presence in my life. I would think that it was dumb of me to leave and he sucked me back in to forgive him and that if I just changed this one little thing the problem would go away. This is the low vibration of taking responsibility and absorbing the manipulative guilt put on by others. I took all of our problems upon myself and he fed me that lie. It took me until the seventh year and eighth attempt to move out. The only way I knew I would stay away was if I signed a lease and packed all my things and moved out and never looked back.

During that time with Lance my responsibilities didn't go away. They just shifted. I was in charge of making half the household income, buying groceries and alcohol, cooking dinner every night, doing the laundry, cleaning the house, keeping up my appearance to please my partner. And God forbid if my nails were naked or chipped and I went out wearing flats. Wearing high heels gave me rewarding attention and I was expected to look like a chic, rich person.

This relationship wasn't a partnership, it was manipulation, and control, and I was innocent and gullible enough to think it was true love. In the final arguments he divulged to me that he picked me specifically for that gullible quality. I was easy to control and shape into whom he wanted.

The heartache came from the constant cycle of state of Lance's disappointment or boredom. And he always blamed me, it was my responsibility to make him happy and keep things exciting. And when I didn't want to do something that he wanted me to do he would make me feel uncomfortable and guilt me into trying it. He also would retaliate and do physical things that may not be perceived as physical abuse, but they were subtle ways. Locking me out in the rain, pinning me against the wall, shoving me down on the floor, and in the end slapping me in the face. I didn't deserve to be treated that way, but I didn't see it clearly as an outside bystander. He would be so loving and tender with me most of the time, so when he did I just concluded, based on his insinuating and my people pleasing modus operandi, that I did something wrong to upset him. Guilt was his biggest tool to control me. Lance always knew if he said something mean about me, told me what he wanted me to do, and then pout I would feel so horrible I would give in every time. I didn't even consider my own self sovereignty of my body. I didn't have that self esteem, or self confidence to resist this guilt trip.

- **LISTEN TO ME!**

Men and women young and old, you are a badass! No matter what you think, you are beautiful, unique and powerful. Thank yourself and your body for how spirituous it is, and own your self sovereignty. You are allowed to say "No." And anytime you feel uncomfortable, if you are finding yourself in a situation with somebody whom you may really like, but they are not respecting your body and your soul, then they are not listening to your boundaries, and therefore they are not respecting you. Don't allow them power over you so they make you feel guilty with their words or their actions. Or make you feel like you're worth nothing and you're a loser if you don't do what they want.

- First of all, that's not you. Their feelings are not your fault, and you are not the loser. They don't know how to deal with the rejection or not getting their way.
- They don't know even how to take no for an answer because maybe their parents gave them everything they wanted as a child. And so when they don't get something from someone else, they don't know how to react. So the ego just immediately attacks.
- When you say "No" you are making a healthy choice for yourself and the other party.
- Healthy lovers are able to talk and laugh and joke and grow and communicate through the process of being intimate. No matter if it's actual sex or not even sex.

Have I made myself very clear? You have self sovereignty over your body. To say "No" is your right and you have the power. You deserve someone who can respect you and be able to easily, and with no offenses taken, move along and be flexible to what you're comfortable with and your wishes.

Lance & I's relationship didn't start out as the heartache cycle that it became. It was a gradual process, and when circumstances appeared that forced him to be bored, rejected etc. it brought out that inner child that was so wounded and angry in him. And I was operating from my wounded and conditioned inner child that pleased everyone to keep the peace and receive the love. I did not have the self confidence to put a stop to it sooner. I had the palpable fear of no one else loving me that kept me in this abuse for seven years. We were both codependent.

You have the power to rewrite your subconscious and transform out of your codependent patterns. You will find that once you've broken one codependent relationship, another will become clear to you. I found out most of my relationships, especially with my parents, were codependent. And I had to learn how to draw healthy boundaries in a loving way to eradicate my codependency and love and take care of my inner child as I shared with you in the previous chapter. You can use tools through hypnotherapy, traditional therapy, meditation, and self love exercises. The biggest root to unhealthy connections is the people pleasing element which comes with an open solar plexus. It takes a lot of work and consistency but if you are ready to break free of feeling horrible or dependent or feeling like you just are so sad, and always feeling like you're trying to make sure everyone's happy but yourself, today is that day to regain your self sovereignty back.

Living a life for others and allowing them to drain you of your energy, and self respect is exhausting, and can make you really sick. It drains your energy and it creates dis-ease in your body. That's what I experienced. I was starting to develop a mysterious autoimmune disease that was never diagnosed. I started to not be able to process food that I ate, I would feel bloated, have IBS, and no matter if I eradicated gluten and processed food, I still was ill in the gut. I was ignoring my gut, my second brain, my authority in my Human Design, and there was a lot of stuck negative energy there.

-   **The Answer**

So what is the answer to all my questions : Why did I think those treasures within me were trash? And why did I let so many relationships go and let my current love affair smother my light? How did I get lost? The answer is simple. I did not love myself and embrace myself. I became someone else for love outside of myself. Do you see the catastrophic results when one does this?

You can be programmed and conditioned to be desirable in someone's else's eyes, but at what cost? When you live misaligned with your soul's purpose and light, you suffocate slowly as if you are buried inside a box. You develop dis-ease, you develop depression, addictions, and suicidal thoughts. Those are what I experienced.

If you are not loving yourself more than the other person outside. Then there is something misaligned and unbalanced within yourself. This self love is the opposite of narcissism. Narcissism is created from fear energies and insecurities; from verbal abuse and overindulgence in a person's childhood. It's a mask and a survival mechanism. The self love I speak of is so nourishing you have extra love for others after you've loved your soul deeply. Focus on loving truly, deeply, and breathing in while holding your inner child and loving yourself. Practice the guided meditation below to start your healing process.

***

I never imagined in a million years that I would be groveling in the sand, under the spotlight of the moon in Tahiti. This was not the romantic trip of my dreams; it was the darkest moment in my life.

Treasure lost: My musical practice, my friendships, my sobriety, and the ability to hold healthy relationships.

Main Human Design Element at play: Open Solar Plexus Learn more about Human Design in Chapter 12.

A Gift from the Emotional Toolbox :

I have a couple tools you can start doing right away to start loving yourself and putting up boundaries.

1. Empath Protection Meditation

2. Inner Authority Mantra

Dive Deeper into this topic in S3 Episode 63: Four Tricks Narcissists use to Make Empaths the Problem on the Empath & Narcissist Podcast.

- EMPATH PROTECTION MEDITATION

Practice **Free Empaths Aura Protection Meditation** on Raven Scott Show YouTube channel. "How to Protect your Empath Energy from Negativity. You can access the whole library in the Meditation Playlist.

Here is the transcript:

Find a comfortable place to sit in a quiet space that is private. Close your eyes. Elongate your spine nice, tall or long. Take a deep breath in and a deep breathe out. Place your left hand on your heart and your right hand on your belly. Take a deep breath in again and feel the rise of your belly and chest and out through mouth, ha. Take a deep breath in and out. Ha. ...Now breathe nice and easy now and steady. Relaxed breathing.

And find yourself in a serene quiet location. Your favorite place in nature. It may be a forest, it may be near a body of water, or floating above a stream or on the coast. Take a deep breath in, take a deep breath out. Deep breath in , deep breath out. Continue breathing relaxed.

Sit tall with your spine straight envision a root growing down from your seat bone and base of your spine growing down into the floor. Envision it growing down deeper into the layers of the rock, down through the Earth's layers, down, down, down. Down into the Earth's mantle and rooting and grabbing onto a crystal in the magma of the Earth's core. Imagine that crystal sending white light back up your root connected from magma to your spine slowly shining. Watch the white light travel slowly up the root, up, up, up. Up through the layers of the Earth, up, up, up. Up through the floor and into the base of your spine. Up, up, up, . See the light travel up your spine through each chakra one chakra at a time. Up your root, up through your sacral, up your spine as it passes your abdomen, up your spine see the white light travel up through your heart space , travel up your spine see the white light travel up through your throat. Watch the light travel up through your skull and shine up and out through the top of your head space. And envision the light pouring like a gentle stream of light and then fall down like water over your whole being.

Sit and soak in the light shining and falling all around you over your body. …

In your environment and safe space, now envision yourself surrounded by this white light shower and it has formed a bubble around your whole body down to where you sit. The white light is pouring love, protection, and healing all around you. Sit in this bubble. Notice you can see out, while being hugged by this white light. Notice you can see holes in the bubble that allow you to interact with the outer world, but it blocks the negative. No bad energy may enter your bubble. No guilt, no manipulation, no complaining, it all bounces off the white light bubble and only your inner light can pour out. Your bubble is your screen. Sit inside your screen and lock in the grounding and protection it provides. …

As you sit inside the screen, invoke your protectors and guides from the multidimensional plane. Repeat after me in your head. "I ask and invite, Beloved God, the Divine Mother Earth, Divine Father Sky, Stellar Centers, Maha Avatars, Avatars, Ascended

Master, Spirit Guides, Angels, Arch Angels, Healed Ancestors, call any out by name, all my teachers and only those entities of light, come and be with me. Present yourself, step forward I am here, I am waiting." Wait...

You may see them, you may feel them, you may see colors or words, just trust your experience.

Now tell them "Show me your message, guide me through this life, and present to me divine and clear signs. Guard me against the darkness and negative energies. Let me trust that I am protected and loved. Change me into someone who is fully loving and light. Let everything that needs to repel, repel, and what needs to attract, attract. Thank you. I am you, you are me, we are One."

Sit in the space of receiving for a bit. ...

As you bring your awareness back to this Earth plane, take a deep breath in, and a deep breath out. Deep breath in , deep breath out. Deep breath in, deep breath out. Listen for any final messages Source wants to share with you before you move on with your day. ...

Thank your guides for showing up and giving you your message. Tell them to freely come and go as they wish.

Wiggle your toes. Wiggle your fingers. Start blinking your eyes to bring yourself back to the present and into your body. Take another breath in the present and thank yourself for this practice. Know that you are now grounded, and protected against the dark energies and entities that will try and suck your empath soul dry.

Shine on Beautiful.

Namaste.

- INNER AUTHORITY MANTRA

I am light. I am love, I am calm, confident and powerful. I am protected. I allow what the Universe brings in my life, and I repel what is not healthy for my soul's journey. I am one with the Divine, what needs to come, come. What needs to go, go.

6. FORCES THAT DRIVE NARCISSISM

"**P**lease, please don't leave me. I'll do anything. Don't walk away." I pleaded. Lance replied, "Look at you. You're pathetic." he turned and walked down the shore. I curled into a ball on my knees in the sand, sobbing as if I'd lost him forever.

- **Bottom of the barrel**

In the middle of the night on a romantic trip as newlyweds, Lance was again disappointed in my performance in the bedroom. In reality his extraordinary expectations were not met yet again. We were drunk, partying and my tiny body couldn't stay alert enough. The adrenaline of him leaving me and hating me woke me up quickly.

I was lost, beyond all psychological belief. He was my whole world. I was isolated from my friends and family. I focused all my energies and attention onto him. On my knees on the shore in Tahiti, in the middle of the night, I had reached the bottom of my barrel. I had nothing left to give, no other ways to fix this, and my soul was numb. As I begged for forgiveness and for him to not leave me, I felt utterly hopeless and abandoned by the only person I had in my life. After I sobbed for a while on the shore, I drug myself back to the porch of our suite on the beach. This place should have brought us happiness and laughter. But all it did was hold space for our toxic, codependent patterns. That night, I gave up. A part of myself died and I wanted to finish my body off and drown myself in vodka. I attempted to finish the whole bottle so I could end my suffering once and for all. *What is the point of living anymore, he doesn't love me and I can never keep him happy, and I can't fix our problem.* Is what I thought. This was it, this was the end, I had nothing to lose.

I reached my lowest point because I valued his approval over my life. He was right, I was pathetic. I had fallen from grace, abandoned my family and friends, allowed myself to be sucked into this toxic pattern and the confident leader that I once was, had left.

I ignored all the signs that I was in a toxic relationship, and I put my worth into this one person's hands. I didn't value my own opinion, I didn't have the courage to believe anyone but him, and my mind was all twisted up and confused. I wanted to die, to fade into the ocean and end this insanity. I did the best drinking that I could before I passed out on the porch.

I believed the lies in my head and that he fed me. And what he said to me brought me to a place I never thought I would ever be. I drank and drank all alone while I waited for his return. I drank past the point of nausea, and somehow I passed out. I was ready to die on that porch. I woke the next day with the biggest nauseating hangover I would ever experience in my life. That was my first, and last attempt in killing myself.

- **The wolf in sheep's clothing**

The definition of Narcissistic Personality Disorder according to Wikipedia : **Narcissistic personality disorder (NPD)** is a personality disorder characterized by a long-term pattern of exaggerated feelings of self-importance, an excessive craving for admiration, and struggles with empathy.[1]

"Narcissistic Personality Disorder (NPD) is characterized by a persistent pattern of grandiosity, fantasies of unlimited power or importance, and the need for admiration or special treatment." - National Library of Medicine

According to those definitions and what we all assume when we think of a narcissist is someone that is too sure of themselves. Someone who could never be hurt or is afraid of anything. They are so full of themselves they never experience worry, pain, or doubt and only project control and unhealthy love for one's self. However, according to Dr. Ramani, a clinical psychologist who specializes in narcissist disorder, "It's the opposite of self love. They are people with no empathy, are grandiose, feel deeply entitled, arrogant, and can't handle frustration." Disappointment is devastating to them and when they are faced with it they become either enraged or depressed. In turn they project their rage out onto their victim so they do not have to carry it.

Looking back, this was Lance. Unknowingly, I found myself in a relationship with a narcissist. I didn't know while I was in the midst of this insane nightmare. And at my lowest all I felt was I was falling too deep into this black vortex. I could see it when I closed my eyes. After my close encounter with the voices in my head wanting to end this life, I felt that was the turning point for me. I realized I had die to my weak self that was trapped and I was going to find my way out of this vortex and it wasn't going to be how I had been approaching things all along. I wasn't dealing with a clinically sane person. You can't win an argument with a narcissist. They are expert mind twisters to make sure they never appear or feel wrong.

At the beginning, as an empath, I would sense that he couldn't handle it subconsciously and to appease and stop the tension or argument I would take on his burden or the blame. I constantly humbled myself as I was taught as a good Catholic, and I allowed him to have the win. The problem comes when I did this over and over again, the pattern was set and he slid in and took advantage of my humility. He depended on my energy for his praise and approval and he learned to feel good with me around. So in turn to ensure he wouldn't lose me as that perfect martyr, he manipulated me to be his devoted punching bag.

- **Three Types of Narcissists**

Covert Narcissists -They are the quiet victimized types. They believe the world never saw how great they were. They are angry at the world, sullen, and look depressed. When they are triggered they get very angry and dangerous, and they will go off on you lecturing or yelling for what feels like hours. Nothing goes their way and then they are bitter and vengeful. Think of the Joker from Batman. His life didn't go as he expected every step and he was passionate to seek revenge.

Malignant Narcissists- They are grandiose and charming. They manipulate, lie, cheat, spie, black mail and steal to gain an advantage over people. They are dangerous and are on the last thread of their psyche before they become a psychopath.

Noble Narcissists - They are narcissists that do lots of good things in the name of charity for validation. The great beautiful philanthropist or humanitarian. They do it so grandiose that they get their name on a building. Or they will through what they have done for you in your face to show you how they are the hero versus the villain. They look really good on the outside rescuing, but at home behind closed doors, they are cruel to their families.

Very few people have the diagnosis. 1-4% are diagnosed. Narcissism is more common than that and is more of an adjective.

Narcissism is not genetic, it is a conditioned state from childhood. Their lack of emotional support and intelligence instills in the child this unhealthy coping mechanism. They either have parents who are narcissists themselves and they pick up the habits and/or they have very distracted parents. They are overindulged and get whatever they want physically, but their emotional needs are completely undernourished. And the parent isn't available when they are sad or scared. They only get value for what they do and they feel no one cares about their inner self and soul and only what they do on the outside is where they receive the love and recognition. This will start to emerge at 17 or 18 as they start to relate to others romantically and step into their own identity and there is nothing you can fix, once they've reached that age. This pattern is not changeable. Narcissists can't be fully cured. They are on the very bottom scale of emotional intelligence and at best you can help them, by drawing a boundary that they must go to therapy. And they must not stop going to therapy for many years, and they will change only if they are willing to bring their emotional intelligence up a few levels on the scale. This ultimately is a choice.

They believe they can do no wrong, ever. Their parent has never scolded them. It's everyone else's fault. It's never the child's to blame, which is unhealthy in the development of process because you need to teach responsibility in conflict. The real truth is everyone in every conflict, has contributed in some way. There's always two sides to the argument. Even if one side smaller than the other, there's always something to take responsibility for and to apologize for; improve and correct, and evolve and be a better person.

And when someone doesn't receive that in their early development years, and they're spoiled and, they're loved like a partner by their parent. It creates a very toxic self identity and entitlement to things in the world.

They have experienced trauma in their life. This is a questionable and a dangerous thought to consider for you empath, because it opens up the door for sympathy that initiates you to pity them and try to help them. I would argue that four children could experience trauma and yet only one, as a result, becomes a narcissist. There is a choice to live in integrity, or live evil centered.

"I have never come across a trauma survivor who sucks all the air out of the room and all the attention in the room who vacuums all the attention to them. I have never come across a trauma survivor who feels entitled. To treat people like objects. I have never come across a trauma survivor who takes advantage of people's weaknesses and their positive qualities and personality traits.

I've never come across a trauma survivor who intentionally pushes buttons in people to elicit reactions and then targets them using those reactions. I have come across people, trauma survivors, real trauma survivors, who are convinced that they deserve to be punished, that they seek permission to even breathe the oxygen in a room.

No. Trauma does not make you an ass hole. I can understand that trauma changes your brain and, coping mechanisms and defenses and everything related psychological trauma, but I can't make sense of this stark difference that those who have chosen the dark path have chosen to be assholes to others."

-Danish Bashir @narcabusecoach

7 Red Flags Of A Narcissist

The most common phrase and kiss of death that you are in a relationship with a Narcissist.

- *"Noone is ever gonna love you the way I love you."*

And boy did I hear that like a broken record in my relationship. I fell into the trap of the Narcissists abusive pattern.

Narcissists win their prospective partners over by making them feel they are the center of the Universe. They love-bomb you. They capture you with attention, gifts, praise, and adventures. It's a game to them. Narcissists are master manipulators so as they are showering you with love, they are receiving your love and praise in return and using it as fuel to bolster themselves up. And they will bring it back up in times of an argument to remind you how well of a lover they are.

Once the love bombing is sufficient and you have emotionally committed or even physically moved in with them, you are now captured in their pattern. Then they set you aside on their shelf as a trophy. They forget to love you and treat you right, and start to control you and mold you into whom they desire. They do this with a push and pull emotional game of tug of war. They can easily shine light on you and make you feel adored and then in the blink of an eye discard you and give you the silent cold treatment or other abusive behaviors. They are very good at dating and courtship and the love bomb is just that, a process that everything happens too fast.

The following are signs you are in a relationship with a narcissist and are emotionally abused. If any of them sound familiar do not ignore these warning signs and seek professional help immediately.

- 1. Constantly seeking validation.

"Look how great I am.

Look at my car.

Look how I'm dressed.

Look how smart I am."

This is what the narcissist giant child is craving and shouting to the world as an adult through their actions. In my situation, it was all about Lance. I saw him as my Savior and my ticket out of the middle class and my desires overcame my intuition. He looked handsome with both supermodel mom and grandmother, and a professional baseball player for a father. He drove a nice Porsche convertible, which he took better care of than he cared for me. He dressed in nice leather shoes, button down shirts and nice slacks; the veritable country club look. He always showed off his jeopardy-like skills with facts and things, and every time I ogled at how smart he was, he would adore the praise and say, "Awe, Ray" in a condescending and doting voice at the same time. The tone was you're so cute and will never be as smart as me, you are rewarded for praising me.

The world and our relationship revolved around him. We did what he liked, dined where his taste buds liked, and we listened to what he chose. I just had to either like it and go along (which I did) or not go at all. I am an easy going person that puts the needs of others before me, this is one of the reasons he chose me. He didn't ask about me, he didn't ask what kind of music that I wanted, or ask if I was too tired that night for sex. He never really cared to learn my deepest thoughts and desires. He didn't listen to me for very long and every response he had to my dreams and ponderings was what his thoughts were about how they were invalid. He believed his thoughts were the only correct thoughts and he could talk for hours about himself and his ideas. If I was on board, then it was just enjoyable light listening, however if I wasn't he would talk and lecture until I came around to believe in his idea. He was relentless to make sure I was always believing what he did. This is how he controlled me. Deep questions of what I want as a person, the topics of desires, dreams and future were not questions, but assumptions that his would be met and mine didn't matter. With him I felt it wasn't an option to explore what I was passionate about and change anything. And I was too in awe, and felt too undeserving, that I went along with it all, even if deep down I was open or flexible to the possibilities of what he wasn't open to. My self esteem was so low I felt my hopes and dreams were not worthy of manifesting. I was still punishing myself from my past failures, pressure of being responsible and believing the false narrative that I was worthless.

I looked up to him and his family, so I was in learning and people pleasing mode. I went along with the flow, enjoyed the different experiences than I had growing up, and I was blinded by desire to this warning sign. However, the danger was that I buried myself, my talents and desires for the achievement of being loved by high class people. I sought status and perceived success over my own internal personal dreams.

He was not shy when it came time to share with me all of his thoughts and beliefs and ideas about how everything works in the world and how everything should be, and how a woman should look and act and be. This was again reinforcement that everyone must be what he wants as it is all about his opinions. This also was his opportunity to subconsciously reshape and control me. It was no secret, and quite obvious, when we first met I was the granola girl as I mentioned earlier. And he set me up to meet his mother and grandmother, both glam women and retired models on an awards night. The first time I met his mother it was at her home to watch the Academy Awards show. He had zero desire to watch the awards with them, and I'm sure he never had in the past, however he had a plan. He planned on me seeing them and bonding with them over a fashion oriented show and I would myself inquire about dressing and looking like them. It worked like a charm, as a master manipulator he had me begging his mom to do a makeover on me the next day. And after that makeover the rest of our seven years together I played the role of the beautiful glam girl.

My style was a submissive girlfriend, "What can I get for you. You work so hard. What can I do for you." Even when the true fact was I was the one who worked hard on my feet in heels all day selling and talking to people, while he sat in his chair at the computer for half the day and woke up late around 11 AM. I would work all day, come home and cook and clean up solely on my own while he continued to do what he desired at the computer or watch TV. There was no teamwork, only I held responsibility for the whole housework. Then after all that I would relax with my cocktail and I would take on the responsibility again to be the hot girlfriend and I allowed him to "pleasure me" way past when it was pleasurable for me. Then I would be tired, and disconnected and he would in turn blame me for not being able to be sufficient for his pleasures.

Can you see the pattern? With the Narcissist, it is all about them.

I ignored that he was all about himself and put him on a pedestal and enabled and praised him for being a genius, and all knowing. He knew best in my eyes.

- 2. Narcissists are hypersensitive and paranoid

Narcissists are very controlling, because they are deeply insecure. They subconsciously strategically lock in and capture insecure people, people pleasures, from tough family backgrounds, or from loving households. The people pleasers are very common amongst women. Especially us empathic women, we feel we have to do our part, keep harmony, and earn love through making others happy. Those with rough backgrounds have a deep insecurity in themselves as well and believe they are worthless. People from really happy families fall for Narcissists because they believe love can cure everything and take on as their personal duty to heal and fix their partner.

He didn't care to meet or get to know my family. It was all about his family and going over to his house and driving his car and doing things his way. When he picked me up for dates, when I lived at my parents house, he would text or honk. He didn't come up to the door. I ran to not stir up any unrest or conflict. But what this showed him was I didn't respect my family or myself enough for him to take the effort to park the car, get out and knock and go through cordial motions. He told me he was above that, that mundane socializing was useless.

He became more and more paranoid once we left our friend group at church. No one could be trusted. He remained friends with one person and that person had deep secrets as well, so the friendship was activity based only while each discussed nothing deep. When things became tumultuous, therapy was out of the question. And we never ventured out and always ate at the same restaurants and he had a very rigid routine.

He would share with me he hacked into mine or a friends account to spy on them, for very minor reasons. He would have tricks and hacks that allowed him to know others comings and goings. He would always hint he had tabs on me as well, the streak of control. I thought his tricks were clever at first, but then they started to scare me. And realize he could spy into my email at any moment, I had zero privacy from him and that was his element of control.

The paranoia of new people and opening themselves up to uncontrollable situations is a real fear. If he couldn't figure out and have an exit route or excuse, he would not go or do that activity. He never would let another drive him, he was never a passenger, and always the driver.

Opening up to new relationships was not an option in his mind. He encouraged me to distance myself from my family and would not make new friends with any of my friends. The only mutual friend we had was his best friend whom I was allowed in to meet him after a couple years. The less people involved in our relationship and my life the easier it was on him. It was very subtle but he fed my fire of anger toward them and he insulted them and talked poorly about them in our private home. He didn't know or meet them but one time. After that he wanted nothing to do with them. They were very nice to him and not rude at all. When I was angry with them and hurt and I didn't want to talk to them, he wasn't the wise conscious man I needed that should have said, "you should give them another try." He was happy I kept my distance so it was easier to manage my ideas and thoughts. His paranoia grew to the point that his only contacts in the world were his family, his best friend, and myself.

By Lance and I's sixth year in our relationship the arguments and conflict did not relent. I was relentless to solve and fix things. I told him he must marry me or I would leave. I thought if he truly loved me he would marry me and we would change and the commitment would create resolve to stop this cycle. I was so naive and wrong. He did not want me to leave, he had collected me, grown comfortable with my forgiveness and codependency. So in order for me to stay he proposed, very unromantically. We did a wedding his way, at the courthouse with no one else. He wanted it to be a confidential ceremony like celebrities do when they want their own privacy. However he was an unknown man with an extremely tiny circle. We did, however, have a wedding reception. This was a must for myself and his mother. I invited my family into our lives again. I thought we had turned a corner and matured. He only put on a show and spent time with them at the end of our relationship. As I matured I realized I wanted to be a wife and have kids. He still had zero desire to be a father. I thought marrying would normalize things, and stabilize our turbulence. Boy was I wrong.

3. - They have a bolstered ego.

The Narcissist will fake their confidence and perfection and invalidate everyone else around them to cover up their insecurities. Remember they were conditioned from a very young age to seek love and approval through performance only. Their sadness, fear, and anger were never acknowledged and dealt with in a healthy way. So in order to sustain their facade that they have no flaws they put others down.

They love praise from others and can talk hours about themselves.

Remember that first time Lance and I met at the summer camp? He could talk for hours about himself and all the knowledge he possessed. I was in awe and didn't see how selfish that was. They are very charming and will share with you all they know about a topic. It seems helpful at first, but when you start to share or have questions about what they think the claws come out.

He would manipulate the scenario to make me feel dumb, wrong, and put in my place. The sharpness of their tongues can cut you like a samurai sword with no time to fight back. I was always stricken with no words to respond because the audacity and overconfidence of his ego was so intense.

He was overconfident in every aspect of his life. The interesting thing is he really was accomplished, except for when it came to emotional matters. He would fake that he was strong and courageous, never showing his vulnerability but one desperate moment when his career had fallen and crashed. He lay on the floor hopeless and wished to die. I loved and cared for this broken little boy that had crawled out of his hiding place. He was devastated and worse it was by his own father. Once I witnessed this I started to awaken to the fact that he needed therapy and his bolstered ego was his defense mechanism to protect his heartbroken and abandoned little inner child.

Always behind one's big bravado is a wounded child screaming to be healed but has been locked in a cage buried in the deep. Narcissists being the classic case.

4. - Forgiveness is the narcissist's weapon.

The morning after every argument the manipulation would lay on thick. I as the empath would feel terrible we even had an argument and I took on the responsibility for it and the blame. He didn't apologize, correct me and tell me it was his fault as well, he leaned in and poured on the guilt. My flaw and pattern was that I would forgive him before he would ever need to say "I'm sorry." And he then would not apologize. And we would take long walks and talk over how I could change to fix our problem. He used my leniency against me as a weapon to keep me coming back for more. I believe he was consciously doing this mind trick as the most dangerous tactic of all. He would remove love from me and wait for me to run into his arms for help and forgiveness for his wrong doing.

On the outside looking in this is obvious emotional abuse. However in the midst of this cyclone I found rhythm and dependence on this pattern. I had so much hope that the next fix would be the cure. When in reality, it was just thousands of bandaids on the wrong wound, and the gaping hole of the real injury was bleeding out. I was the body who was bleeding dry, my soul sucked a little more out from me, and I fell into the dark vortex centimeter by centimeter every day.

Emotional abuse includes verbal abuse; intimidation and terrorization; humiliation and degradation; exploitation; harassment; rejection and withholding of affection; isolation; and excessive control. I personally experienced most of these. Towards the end he became physically intimidating once his words didn't have power in my mind. He pinned me against the wall once proving his power over me. He pinned me on my belly once and commenced to force himself on me to prove I was weak and no defense against a rapist, and he locked me out in the cold rain. Humiliation and degrading was an almost daily occurrence when I would be tired or passed out after four hours of sexual intercourse he insisted on having. The mere act of our intimacy was exploitation. He made it into such a big "party" every time serving me drink after drink to "loosen me up" so he could gain sexual pleasure. I remember watching a movie where a prostitute was attacked and they show the scene and then her in the shower after the men left. I remember knowing exactly how she felt, the feeling of having no choice and feeling that violation the next day. There is a difference between intimacy between lovers and exploitation to gain one parties pleasures. I had only experienced the latter and I was unaware until I left. This form of exploitation was also diagnosed that I had encountered sexual abuse. His ego was so self serving that he guilted me into what he wanted. The requests were often for his pleasure in bed. Not stopping to consider if I truly was desiring, nor could he tell because my judgement was clouded with alcohol. The amount of hours, and positions and places were not fun after a couple, but it was my duty to shut up and put up otherwise he would withdraw his love from me. True consent is not under the influence of alcohol. This is well known in legal realms.

The abuse didn't feel like rape or abuse because I did consciously consent and was in a consensual relationship. But had I had confidence, courage, clarity, and not been under the influence of alcohol I would've stopped the whole process hours earlier. He would have become mad, and then I would have left and the end of that. This is what healthy self sovereignty looks like. However this sexual abuse and disappointment led to rejection. It was a multi-day occurrence during the week that he would not talk to me for the first half of the day or longer the next morning. He also would remove planned trips or gifts he had given me. I've already shared about how isolated I was, and the need for him to control everything in our lives. There was no desire in his

Narcissistic Ego to apologize or change, he was set in his way and he was always going to desire what his needs were over mine.

I loved him very much, and he loved me how he was equipped to with his limited emotional maturity. However, that love did not heal his wounds and our toxic relationship. Love does not cure all. Therapy and willingness to admit you are wrong are the first steps before love and energy healing can transform someone.

I was so desperate to be loved, but at what cost?

5. - Master Manipulators

Narcissistic abuse creates doubt and codependency in the other person's mind, every decision is full of uncertainty and you are always consulting the narcissist to make decisions for you. This is how they train you. You may not have entered the relationship powerless. However their games and manipulation slowly eats away at your confidence and power.

Guilt trips were constant. It was very subtle and I wish I could have recognized it. But again I felt low-class and my self-worth was at a zero, and not having enough experience with boys made me feel I didn't really deserve anybody. I was just grateful for who I had. Emotional abuse aside, I felt I had arrived and elevated my human status. I was very grateful that I found someone so tall, dark and handsome and I made excuses for his disrespectful and demeaning comments. He really "looked like a cool drink of water but he was candy coated misery." - Carrie Underwood

The first red flag I ignored, was at the beginning, I was strong, independent and in my own apartment. One night, the romance started kind of going a little bit weird. He pushed beyond my boundaries of comfort and urged me to try it. His tone of voice made me feel like I'd be an idiot if I didn't go on with his urging. I should have put the brakes on it, and stood up for my self respect. My body was saying no, but my people-pleasing gave in. Another instance of his defined will took over my open will center. He backed off for a bit with that type of activity as he sensed I did not like it and I was in a position I could break it off and still be independent. Once he drew me in closer to depending on him and I moved in with him, he then tried those things again. And I gladly took it at that time because he groomed me to be more adventurous and he made it sound enticing and sexy. And while those things are in a healthy relationship, this felt as if I was pleasing him after a while and honestly was work. I didn't feel connected or intimate, I felt like a play thing and a commodity.

I must share a bit of advice, no matter how much guilt is poured on you, just say "no", go, and stay away. The guilt is a clear sign that this person does not respect your boundaries and only cares for their own needs. Guilt is different from a request or conversation about a new adventure. Guilt involves one party on board, while a new adventure involves both parties excited to try.

Another way they manipulate is you feel you need to have a tape recorder capturing your conversations. His words were perfectly calculated to make me confused. I would constantly feel as if I were crazy. I would come to him with a clear idea and leave as if that idea were thrown out the window, run over by a bus, reshaped, and then held in my arms as my own. And everytime I was stunned and confused then in full resolve to his case or idea.

This constant heartache was wearing on me, and I would consult with my friends at work. They would see me hurting emotionally and want to try and help, as any good friend should. They were so right that he needed to treat me with love and respect. And every time I would bring this case to him, and stand up for myself he would get to the bottom of where this message came from. I would admit I talked to my friends and he would tear apart my friend's character, integrity, and idea.

He then pitted me against my friends, just as he did my family, and I would be mad at them and I would come back to them telling them to stay out of my business. They saw right through his abusive manipulation, and would separate themselves from me, or they would in turn try and argue with me and we would split up as friends hurt and offended. His motives as an insecure narcissist were simple, he was focused on controlling his environment and if I had friends that kept telling me he was not good for me, then I would leave him and his play puppet would be gone.

After this occurrence happened all throughout our relationship, and once I left I had no friends with the exception of my new roommate. This tumultuous cycle would make me feel like I was taking crazy pills. One side of my brain would understand logically I am not being treated as I deserved, and then I would come back to Lance, and he would convince me back into the idea that he was the one who knew how things were. I was very isolated and depressed and leaned on alcohol to get me through these crazy times.

They are masters at gas lighting. This makes one doubt one's reality. The term comes from the movie Gas lighting - where the main character would adjust the gas light in the house high to low while his co host would not be looking. She would question him if he changed the lights. He would deny it and answer, no. It's a bit of a twilight zone type movie where the co host went crazy in the end because he kept messing with the lights and lying about it. Narcissists do the same thing to put up the front they are perfect. They will say "You're being too sensitive" denying someone's emotions rather than taking responsibility. They deny someone's experience, in order to maintain control and confident presence. From my experience, it felt as if I was living in a house of mirrors, but none of the reflections were mine. They were of him, his constructs, his ideal women, and his puppet.

The other way he manipulated me was when I would be mad and hurt and leave to stay the night at a family member's home away from him, I felt the need to reach out and write a really long text or email explaining myself because he just wouldn't listen. But he didn't want to understand my feelings or side of the story. He would reply back with a kind and authoritative role that he understood I missed him. And if I would just come home we could figure it out. I would then pack up all my things again and go back home the next day.

You may get another response from a narcissist and I didn't receive this until he knew I was resolved to never return. They will reply with a very toxic and accusatory response and make you feel wrong for your viewpoint. It's infuriating, and the more you respond in trying to clear your story and make your point they dig you in a deeper and deeper hole in their darkness. There is no reasoning with them, they will never take responsibility and they will deflect the blame all on you. It's best to be silent and not feed the self-centered monster.

6. - Narcissists Lack Empathy

They just don't care about others. Due to their self survival skills of always achieving or appearing successful, they do not have time or the ability to care about others. They were never taught the emotional muscle of empathy in their childhood. Their parents were either distracted, in a mess themselves, or over-indulged them. They also appear very distracted and may blame ADD. However they have no problem talking about themselves for hours. They cannot be bothered with others' feelings and musings. They don't care to listen when the conversation isn't about them. They take and take and take, and just don't care to give back.

Lance punished me for not being sexy enough by canceling vacations he planned. He had zero empathy for how that made me feel. If I wasn't meeting his needs, he treated me as if pleasing him was rewarded, rather than bonding. He would say things as if his motivation was to please me in bed, however he had no radar or willingness to accept that after hour two of sex I didn't want to be pleased anymore. His facade of pleasing me, was for his enjoyment, not mine. And when I was done, over it, tired, dried up, or passed out, it was my fault. As if I was some porn star Barbie toy that was broken. He didn't ever ask or tell me that he was fine to just snuggle because I had a long day at work. We did have nights where that was the case, but the stage was set for the unspoken activity to occur every time he took me out to dinner. It only took one time he showed his anger towards me, was all the message I needed to know this was the way of things as he expected. As mentioned above, the length of time of the activity was not very considerate to my schedule the next morning. Friday nights were party nights for him, however I worked every Saturday morning early and there was no consideration for how much sleep I needed before. Even though it was my choice, I also was avoiding an argument and feeling his disappointment by partying with him. Those Saturday mornings I visually looked hungover and felt like a fish out of water. Sluggish, short of breath, and feeling so exhausted. I was so deep into the relationship at that point that I still didn't want to believe that he was not being healthy or kind, or even the right person for me. I truly believed this was how life landed for me, it sucked on Saturdays and other days, and I was resigned to this way of life.

Accusing others for a mistake is another way they lack empathy. This puts the other person in the relationship in a position to defend themselves. Rather than have vulnerability and grace and apologizing, they accuse, project and blame others for minor infractions. This lack of emotional intelligence can be exhausting for the receiver and not a healthy way to interact.

For instance, they may make a minor mistake as most humans do, and you ask what happened out of curiosity and they go off on you and accuse you of how you are the source of the mistake in a roundabout way. And you are left to take the abuse of defending yourself that you don't do whatever they've just accused of you. The emotional healthy response would be, "Oh, ya, sorry I broke the piece trying to fix it. I will buy another one." This shows taking responsibility, which the narcissist will never do, and an apologetic response not blaming anyone, and acknowledging it was an honest mistake that is normal among human beings.

Once I was in my Saturn Return and had my awakening I wasn't truly aware of how dismissive he was of my feelings. It happened throughout the whole seven years, however it was very clear one night, near the end, I shared with him a beautiful trip and experience I had that was filled with joy. He did not acknowledge how wonderful that was for me; he immediately dismissed my feelings and went on and on about how those people whom I just visited were wrong people, and my feelings and experience were invalid. I excused myself from the dinner table, as we were out in public, I went into the bathroom and sobbed my panic out. I realized after seven years, he was never going to hear me or care for my happiness.

7. - It is Very Invalidating to be in Their Presence.

When with a narcissist, whether it's your parent, partner, or sibling, it's very invalidating to be in their presence and this puts you in a very dangerous situation. You are manipulated and sucked into their aura, yet while you are in it they are spewing darkness and sucking your light out of you for themselves to shine brighter. It is important to draw boundaries with this type of person in your life.

With Lance, when I spoke up for my own feelings and thoughts I was invalidated, dismissed, and lectured for it.

A healthy relationship allows for conversations that allow you both to express your thoughts and feelings with little to no judgement. An opposing opinion that is coming from respect is healthy, and is completely different from a narcissist angle to control, coerce, and tear down your identity and feelings for their gain. The healthy debate should be done with respect and bureaucracy. And in the end you may agree to disagree. With narcissists they will die on their hill of opinion, or more likely they will sacrifice you on their debate hill and leave you for dead feeling bolstered up and their ego pumping it's chest. A healthy relationship may have one partner exploring and questioning while the other holds space for them to do so, giving them space and grace to find their own answer. In a relationship with a narcissist, you have zero space and grace for questioning ideas, and until you agree and are back in their manipulated control and they feel comfortable you are on their side, they will not rest or give you space to find your own answers. In a healthy relationship you may come to a compromise. In a relationship with a narcissist, they don't know what compromise is, they get what they get always and will take it from you at all costs. They are used to getting their way all the time, so they do not know how to compromise.

In my circumstance with Lance, he made it his life's purpose to prove me wrong, convince me that his way was right, and I was stupid for thinking of a new idea outside of his control. I was eventually convinced his view was the correct one and with my open will center I adopted his will and ideas as my own. I lost many friends this way, sacrificed myself, lived an inauthentic life, and felt as if I was spinning in a washing machine. This is how a defined will center (Lance) and an undefined will center (me) can potentially interact at their lowest frequencies.

I understand that having the courage and self love to speak up for one's beliefs and self sovereignty may be the biggest challenge for one to master. If you have been silent and quiet and trying to please the narcissist, and are codependent you will find it takes practice. Your biggest challenge is getting the courage to disagree and walk away when the other person invalidates you. It takes victims in an abusive relationship on average twelve attempts to leave. So give yourself grace and know you have courage to leave, because you have more courage to stay in a hurtful situation. The Divine will guide you and take care of every step when you find resolve. It was the easiest process when I put my faith in something greater than me when I stepped out into the dark abyss of the unknown without him.

I will share a tool at the end of this chapter on how to clear that stuck energy in your throat, self, or heart chakra. For most of us that are quiet people pleasers, we have a lot of stuck energy in our throats. It stops us from speaking up and manifesting a situation that is safe and honoring our human experience. Open up your throat chakra if you have that struggle of your throat chakra closing. This chakra healing meditation will be listed at the end of the chapter.

Healing, Trusting, Standing In
Your Power, & Letting Go

No matter how low you get, or how long your thoughts and fears may imprison you in depression, heartbreak, or thoughts of uselessness, you must become aware those are not true. You can free yourself. How are you talking to yourself? Are you self deprecating? Are you insulting yourself? Believing you are not worth it? Feel as an imposter? Like you don't deserve it? Do you tell yourself you are dumb?

"I'm such an idiot!" I used to say to myself all the time, even after

I left Lance and was blessed with a new life with an amazing man and children. But I stopped once I realized that everything I do my children catch and copy. I realized my self degradation is the number one reason I fell into a relationship where I allowed myself to be treated with no respect, because I did not have respect for myself.

And it's just so fascinating, as an outside observer of my own life, that I believed that behavior and treatment was okay. That treatment is not what I witnessed in my father. He was such a caring husband and doted on my mother, and did everything that she needed and jumped in and volunteered. He apologized and cried with her and held her. He was very much a prince charming for her. Evidence shows, on the contrary to what logic would dictate, that it is not uncommon for people from a happy household to be caught in the trap of a Narcissist. They get trapped taking the blame and trying to fix the narcissist because they believe love is the ultimate answer to all problems. They were raised on Disney fairytales as I was, and that loving someone outside of yourself is the answer. If that stable loving environment excludes the development of autonomy then their child may still be susceptible. If they are not teaching emotional intelligence and analytical skills to read people's character, then they are vulnerable to the trap of the narcissist. Karma may have led me as well, so I would be able to awaken and contribute to the collective as my Human Design states. I needed to be able to go on the journey so I benefitted towards the greater good of others. Our soul's are on a Karmic journey, always learning and experiencing life in order to evolve and mature.

The difficulty with subscribing to the belief that love and therapy can fix a narcissist is it gives you false hope. The narcissists are operating under a strong subconscious power to cover their insecurity and intentionally sacrifice others to keep themselves "alive." Their behavior is instilled and programmed in them at an early age and through childhood. The pitfall for this vicious cycle is the current culture and world tells the narcissist that they are doing great because they act perfect in public, and they buy into their charm, like a snake by a charmer.

Both parties in this type of relationship get stuck as an addict chasing a high, trying to fix and get the beginning back. As soon as the narcissist feels their lover withdraw and question if this is a good relationship for them to be in, they lay on love bombing part two. Remember in the beginning of a narcissist courtship they are charming and pour the love on their subject. Then once they have secured the lover they stop investing in them and disregard them and stop the act of loving them. After they get comfortable again and their lover flees to get out of the abusive relationship they pour on love bombing part 3, etc. In my case I left seven times and got love bombed after each time to draw me back in. And I stayed in the relationship and crawled back to him. I thought I could fix it, him, and us. I truly thought I could change him. This is unfortunately far too common a pattern. And a tell tale sign you are in an abusive relationship. We still believe in fairytales and love is the cure of all. Music, culture, movies and more always end stories with loving being the transformative cure all. While I still believe love and kindness needs to flow from one person to another like water, it will not cure an extremely broken person. The narcissist is looking for love they never received in their childhood, however you will not be able to fill that hole, because they need that repaired from the first offenders, their parents.

Narcissists usually have really bad back stories but it's not an excuse to treat another with disregard and disrespect.

- DRAWING BOUNDARIES

If you've been enlightened that your partner is a narcissist, it may come to your realization some time sooner or later that one of your parents is also. We typically are comfortable with those patterns because we have been conditioned through childhood. So what do you do when you can't leave this person or they are a parent or sibling? One option is, you could not talk to them. However, if your siblings are gathering with them and you want to be involved in a whole family gathering, you will need to have certain boundaries set up for yourself to communicate and have to protect yourself.

1. You do not need to explain or justify your choices and actions to them. Nor them you. You may want to know why they said something hurtful, but the more you dig the deeper you will be buried in bull crap.
2. You have the freedom to leave at any time it feels unsafe or that you are being attacked or persuaded to "behave".
3. You can tell them, I do not want to talk about this right now, I would like to enjoy the family gathering. And tell them you will talk about it later. And then you can or cannot have the conversation on your own time at your own freedom.
4. You can always agree to disagree and hold fast to your feelings and ideas.
5. Learn to side step intrusive questions and negative

comments . Or call them out on it and ask to please stop saying that.

6. Don't give in to their sales pitch of why they are not taking responsibility for their actions.
7. Good boundaries include consequences.

- **How do you get out?**

It's scary and can be dangerous. I can attest to this from first hand. He had coercive control, he tracked my coming and goings, hacked into my email. He caused fear in me if I left, and fear in me if I stayed. The isolation and dependence made me feel I didn't have a safe place to go anymore. I did not have children in the mix to create more fear for me to protect my children, but I know many men and women have to deal with this. You may need to file a restraining order. It may take years to get out. The mental control may be intense. You may have terrifying fights in custody battles, restraining orders, and the fall out from these situations are immeasurable. You believe the narrative that you are bad, insecure. However, with documentation starting as soon as you can to journaling what happens, your children's journals, neighbor witnesses, other family member witnesses and police reports all can support you in your legal fight for full custody. Remember to clear your browser history on your phone and your computer, or better yet, use a friend's computer so they cannot track your activity. You are brave, you can do it. An inspirational story is of a fellow narcissist abuse coach. She had gone through all her legal rights and had restraining orders against her x, and he would find them over and over and make their life miserable. She finally picked up her life and took the hard leap and moved a whole countryside away in order to finally regain her life back and her children's safety. She was so brave, and when the time comes, you will too. Be careful with your documentation and have a safe neutral person keep it for you, or have a super secure two step authentication for every log in. When it's time to leave, do it where there won't be conflict, in the middle of the night once they are asleep, or call the police or family for assistance to get your things and leave safely.

Have faith.

- **Self Sovereignty**

Self Sovereignty is essential for you to draw healthy boundaries. Growing up Catholic, this was not what I was conditioned to believe. I was raised that God's sovereignty and being codependent on God was the way to Heaven and self sovereignty is selfish and a way a "lost" person acts. However, for those of us who sacrifice ourselves for others, this needs to be said.:

It's your responsibility to say what you need to say to take care of yourself and to bring joy, love and respect to yourself. Others' reactions are not your responsibility, and you cannot take that on.

No one can tell you if you should stay or go. So the clarity comes when you speak up for yourself and then, see how that person reacts. Is that person super excited that you're finally sharing with them what you desire? If they are saying, " yes let's try that! I really want to make you happy because I love you" then they are worth fighting for and you are in a healthy complicated relationship. Or are they saying "Oh that's bull crap you don't really want that. No, what you really want is (fill in the blank of what they want,)" then they don't have the best intentions for you and you must start your process to leave. You may get a mixed reaction out of fear, they may say "I don't agree with that, for these listed reasons.__,__,__." And that leaves you open for a compromise and a choice if you both want to work more on the relationship with a neutral party. Loving yourself, trusting Source and your authority on decision making (which is in your Human Design chart), and working on your inner power in a healthy way, will allow you to witness your bravery that was in you the whole time. You will feel ready to step into a new phase and stage in your relationship, whatever it may be. Don't fear the future, the Universe has special people and circumstances waiting for you. Your soul contracted you to be in this body and with these people and you had a plan for learning a lesson. You have Spirit guides and Guardian Angels all around you not matter if you are aware or not.

- **You are a gift.**

You were once an innocent child. When you were born you were, and still are, a pure light force without gender or race. It's time to love that child and soul. Learn to love yourself and your inner child, as an adult, and nurture yourself. No matter how ugly, lost, desperate you feel, those are all conditional feelings in a trapped existence that doesn't need to remain true. You can break free of your prison. I know I was able to, and I know you are just as able as I. Stop kicking yourself in the butt; there is no need to beat yourself up. You are unique. Your soul is contracted here for a special reason. You are light, you were born pure and have a life theme and purpose, and your life's circumstances and misfortune do not define you.

Caution: if at any point in your situation you feel that you are in danger, please don't wait to seek help. If you feel life is not worth living anymore, seek help immediately from the number below. You may contact your local police office line for advice or someone that is a safe resource.

Here are some statistics to know you are not alone.

25% of women are battered and physically abused by their partner. Emotional abuse is more prevalent averaging 80%. 40% of women & 32% men reported expressive aggression. 41% of women and 43% of men reported coercive control. You are not alone and you certainly are not to blame or be hard on yourself. The average number of attempts to leave an abusive relationship is twelve. Do not feel weak or a failure that you cannot leave.

You are brave for in fact staying, however give yourself a firm commitment to get out.

Contact your local police for resources to get help.

Contact your abuse hotline: **loveisrespect**: 1-866-331-9474.

800.799.SAFE (7233)

Contact suicide hotline: **National Suicide Prevention Lifeline**: 1-800-273-8255 (24/7)

Treasure lost: Joy for life

Main Human Design Element at play: *Open Will Center, Gate 50 Fear of failing to take care of loved ones & responsibilities. My motivation and trajectory of hope transferred to guilt.*

To learn more about Human Design, read chapter12.

Do the three exercises in the next pages to heal and clear out negative energy.

Dive Deeper into this topic in S3 Episode 62: How Relationship with Narcissist Wreaks Havoc in Empaths Life with Nikki Eisenhauer, on the Empath & Narcissist Podcast.

- CHAKRA HEALING MEDITATION

Practice **Chakra Healing Meditation** on Raven Scott Show YouTube channel. You can access the whole library in the Meditation Playlist.

Chakra Healing Meditation transcript:

Find a comfortable place to sit in a quiet space that is private. Close your eyes. Elongate your spine nice, tall or long. Take a deep breath in and a deep breathe out. Place your left hand on your heart and your right hand on your belly. Take a deep breath in again and feel the rise of your belly and chest and out through mouth, ha. Take a deep in and out. Ha. …Now breathe nice and easy now and steady. Relaxed breathing.

Envision a root or roots growing from your tail bone or spine down into the surface you are on. See them root and continue to move deep into the layers of the Earth. Down, down, down, and reaching the Earth's mantle. They grab hold of a glowing crystal in the magma. The light of this crystal shines bright and starts to illuminate your roots. The light travels slowly back up the roots towards your body. Slowly through the Earth's layers, through the rocks, sediment, layers, dirt, foundation, floor and into your roots attached to your body. The white light travels up through your spine and out the top of your head and golden and white sparkling light pours over your head, and rains over your body. As you envision this light showering you, repeat this invocation with me.

" Supreme Infinity, Divine Father Sky, Divine Mother Earth, Avatars, Ascended Masters, Archangels, Holy Angels, Spirit Guides, Healed Ancestors, and all my Teachers (name any specifically by name). Only entities and energies for my highest good are allowed in this space. And with the help of my Higher Self, I invoke for the Divine Light, Divine Love, and Divine Power. Bless me abundantly with Wisdom, Strength, Courage to find power, balance, equanimity, alignment, and the deepest healing on all levels of all my energy bodies.

In my deepest soul's heart in full faith, Thank you. So Be It, and So It Is."

Now start to envision a ring of white light circling around your Root center, at the base of your spine. You may start to feel a warmth or a tingling, or nothing at all. See the white ring circling around the root Chakra and feel how grateful you are for the mobility this area gives you. The grounding allows your body to exist on this planet, and the anchor it provides while you walk. Be grateful for this center providing the magic of reproduction, for the pleasures and joy this chakra provides. Thank it for the security, grounding, and survival it provides. Say to this Chakra "Thank you. I love you."

Now envision a ring of white light, in addition to the ring around your Root Chakra, to start circling your Sacral Chakra, just below your belly button. See the beauty and power of this area of your body. Feel the white light circling and healing the uterus, blood sugar, urinary tract, and adrenals. You may start to feel a warmth or a tingling, or nothing at all. Be grateful for the intimacy this center gives you the opportunity to have. Thank it for the emotions that come to visit, the waves of sorrow, joy, anger, love, these all are beautiful parts of the human experience. Grateful for the boundaries this center allows you to draw, sit in the space that brings you power to say no. Feel the healing and balancing of substances that pull you into addiction: sugar, alcohol, drugs, pleasing others. Allow the power of this Chakra to allow you to trust your intuition. Say to this Chakra "Thank you. I love you."

Now envision a ring of white light, in addition to the ring around your Sacral, to start circling your Solar Plexus Chakra, in the middle of your abdomen. See the beauty and power of this area of your body. Feel the white light circling and healing the stomach, liver, and digestion. You may start to feel a warmth or a tingling, or nothing at all. Be grateful for the energy this center provides you. Thank your higher self for stepping forward in this Chakra versus your Earth Ego or Lower Self. And thank this center for its ability to bring perfection through practice and mastery. Say to this Chakra "Thank you. I love you."

Now envision a ring of white light, in addition to the ring around your Solar Plexus, to start circling your Heart Chakra, in the center of your chest. See the beauty and power of this area of your body. Feel the white light circling and healing the lungs, heart, blood pressure, and immune system. You may start to feel a warmth or a tingling, or nothing at all. Be grateful for the energy this center provides you. Thank you for the beauty and ability to love others and pierce deep into their souls. Thankful for the muscle of hope to carry on for a better outcome or future. So grateful for the ability to have compassion for those who are suffering physically or emotionally. Thankful for this center allowing for flexibility, ebbing and flowing with the tide. Grateful for this chakra to allow this human existence balance in our duties, joy, rest, and fun. Say to this Chakra "Thank you. I love you."

Now envision a ring of white light, in addition to the ring around your Heart, to start circling your Throat Chakra, in the middle of your neck. See the beauty and power of this area of your body. Feel the white light circling and healing the thyroid, neck, ears, respiratory system, and sinuses. You may start to feel a warmth or a tingling, or nothing at all. Be grateful for the energy this center provides you. Thank you for your ability to communicate. So grateful for the manifestation of those boundaries drawn up and through your voice. So grateful for the creativity that can be expressed. Thank you for the healing my voice can bring myself, and others. Thank you for words that carry energy and become things. Say to this Chakra "Thank you. I love you."

Now envision a ring of white light, in addition to the ring around your Throat Chakra adding on to the others, to start circling your Third Eye Chakra, in the middle of your eyes. See the beauty and power of this area of your body. Feel the white light circling and healing the pituitary, hypothalamus, eyes, and nervous system. You may start to feel a warmth or a tingling, or nothing at all. Be grateful for the energy this center provides you. Thank your Third eye for the ability to see and hear the Spirit world, events history to future through clairvoyance. Thank you for my intuition and ability to have the Knowing. I'm grateful for the psychic senses my Third Eye allows me to have. Say to this Chakra "Thank you. I love you."

Now envision a ring of white light, in addition to the ring around your Third Eye Chakra adding on to the others, to start circling your Crown Chakra, a few fingers above your head. See the beauty and power of this area of your body. Feel the white light circling and healing the Pineal Gland and nervous system. You may start to feel a warmth or a tingling, or nothing at all. Be grateful for the energy this center provides you. Thank your Crown for the ability to understand concepts and the intuitive Knowing. Grateful for the consciousness and awareness it brings to your human experience, to learn lessons and adapt and change. Thank you for the ability to have enlightenments that advance and evolve our spiritual experience as souls. Say to this Chakra "Thank you. I love you."

Lay or sit in this silence of all the seven rings circling your chakras healing your body and focus in on the chakra that is most ailing you.

When you are ready, thank Source, Divine Father Sky, Divine Mother Earth, Stellar Centers, Maha Avatars, Ascended Masters, Archangels, Holy Angels, Spirit Guides, Healed Ancestors, and all your teachers.

I am you, we are one, all is well. Thank you. Namaste.

- MIRROR WORK PART 1

Tell yourself compliments in the mirror every day. Say "You're beautiful." "You have a purpose." "You are unique." "You are valued." Say two or three affirmations every day.

If this is too difficult to believe at first, practice visual meditations and remove yourself from your body and realize you are beautiful. This is what I had to do to realize that I was truly worth all I desire, and that I was beautiful. Beauty for my flaws, beauty shining my light inside out.

This is so important I have repeated this exercise in Chapter 8 with in depth instructions.

Because - let's face it, just because you are reading this doesn't mean you are ready for it all. It is here for you to use as a guide throughout your growth process.

-   JOURNAL RITUAL

What are your dreams and desires in a partner?

What elements are negotiable.

What elements are non-negotiable?

Can you honestly say this person fits in your life or is he/she filling a hole you need to tend to yourself?

Journal all of the emotions out. Burn it in a safe stainless steel pot outside and shower the energy off immediately.

What is the reason why you burn it? This will be explained through the concept that thoughts become things, and words can manifest and have energy and power for life to thrive or shrivel. It's important to get the negative emotions and energy out of your mind and body and when you put it onto paper it is now on a conduit that can be transferred up to the Divine. When you burn it you are burning the energy up as a sacrifice and transmuting the energy. It's important to shower and allow the fresh water to wash away any residual energy surrounding your journal.

After you have completed this initial ritual, do so around every consecutive full moon releasing out all your current emotions. This transmutation is incredibly powerful to peel back the layers in your healing process.

7. EMOTIONAL HAVOC

Courage to leave and relationship aftermath

Dear Universe,

I can't stop crying today. Why am I sad on my birthday?! Is it because it's magnifying the fact that I know I am not treated as I deserve by my husband? I received love and birthday wishes from everyone in my life and in my family, and even from Lance. But just saying nothing else and all the other days feeling alone and unloved doesn't cut it. A wish with words without a present, flowers, kiss, hug, or anything romantic in the slightest is not how I deserve to be treated by my husband. I guess I am really struggling even though I put on a good face. If I'm being honest with myself, I dream of a man who loves to caress me, hold me, kiss me, and isn't ashamed to be with me socializing with friends and family, even if he is in a different mindset than them. I care for those people, therefore he should put his best effort to set aside his ego and try and be there with me and make memories with others that are important in my life.

I'm tired of feeling like a single woman to the rest of the world, and am stuck in a committed relationship at home. I should be enjoying my freedoms as a single woman without the responsibilities of a manchild at home isolating himself.

Every time I try to share my feelings he discounts my feelings and I am not heard. How do I fix this? I hate my birthday. There's always pain, I haven't had a happy blissful birthday since my teens. It's my fault, my expectations are low, and I guess I feel guilty they are too exaggerated and from a romance novel that they are not based in reality. He just doesn't care to want to know what I need. If I'm going to be in the world outside of my home a single woman, maybe I should really just be single.

-Ray

"Cuz the girl that you want, she is tearing us apart, cuz she's everything, everything I am not." - Song: Everything I'm Not by The Veronicas

- **Saturn Return**

In Astrology the Saturn Return is an astro transit that occurs when the planet Saturn comes full circle around the Sun and arrives back in the identical spot it resided in at the moment you were born. The window of age this happens is between 28-30 years of age. This is a pivotal moment in your life. You make big decisions during this time. It may be the birth of a child, a move, or a divorce.

Saturn is the planet that rules Karma. Saturn is the ruler of one's sense of duty, discipline, and responsibility, and their physical and emotional endurance during hardships. It is the planet that influences your view of long term planning and forces you to assess your life's trajectory. Karma is the energy that flows around in the Universe. It is not punishment, or pay back, it is the essence of your soul, the life force and energy that flows. Depending on your intentions and actions it can also be a huge blessing or a major life lesson. Karma is neutral. What you put out into the Universe bounces around and comes back to you. Karma is not fixed to just this one time line and life. Hinduism and Buddhism believe that Karma is the sum of a person's actions in past lives and the current life. Your current life is an opportunity to learn more lessons and tune into Source to find your souls' purpose, lessons, and karmic path.

I gained the resolve to move out during my Saturn Return at age twenty eight, after I came back from a divine and rare trip visiting my cousins and their families. Remember I was isolated and during my many years with Lance I did not talk to my family. They were made into the enemy and I cut ties and stopped going to family holidays and more.

During my wedding reception two years earlier, (yes I married in an attempt to rectify our situation.) My aunt mentioned a trip up to Washington in a year or two. I told her to let me know and I would love to come. During our short marriage, I was still unfulfilled, living my life isolated with my partner and without children. We had dated for years, married for a couple and I was ready to start a family, but he wasn't. The night I returned from my trip, we went out to dinner, I was telling him all about how wonderful my trip was, and how the kids were so sweet, and how much joy I felt. In true narcissist fashion, he didn't acknowledge my feelings. Matter of fact he invalidated them and started telling me how having kids is not needed in this world, and how wrong "breeders" are contributing to overpopulation. I excused myself to the bathroom and in the restaurant bathroom stall I broke down and sobbed. I thought "he is never going to hear me; I am never going to have kids if I stay with him." I pulled myself together and finished dinner. That week, I was removed emotionally from him, I snapped back at a comment he made and he grabbed my wrist and squeezed it tight. It started to hurt and after I demanded for him to let go, he squeezed harder. I didn't know what to do to make it stop so I slapped him, and in turn he let go and slapped me back. I knew he had lost it, he had lost control over me emotionally and resorted to physical violence. I didn't recognize the abuse before because it was all words, but I clearly recognized the hitting as unhealthy and crossing my unspoken boundary. We needed help and I needed to move out to feel safe while we did so. After our final argument that evening, I saw a dark mist hovering in the top portion of my bedroom. I found the courage and resolve that I just need to move out and seek third party help if this relationship was going to work. You see, I moved out many times before because of the constant heart ache from his words, and friends would talk sense into me that he was not right for me. I would pack my things after an argument and move into a family member's house, each destination being different each time. I felt so much anxiety and pain being apart from him, that I would always reach out to him in 24 hours and move back in within the week. But that night was different. I made a commitment to myself to sign a lease, so I could not be weak and come back again.

- **The escape**

This was the part that I feared the most, and was the easiest at the same time. I always feared my future without Lance as a deep dark black abyss. But what I wasn't aware of for so long was that staying was sucking me down even deeper down into an energetic dark vortex. The irony of my fear versus what reality was, is clear now.

I had just met an old contact through Lance while signing up for insurance after we married. She and I reconnected and started talking. I shared with her my dilemma and situation and that I wanted to move out so we can work on our relationship through therapy. She connected me with another friend of hers that was in a similar situation and had been living with her x for years and wanted to move out as well.

I knew of an apartment complex my friend years ago encouraged me to move into while amidst my emotional anguish. Her seed she planted remained with me to that day and my new potential roommate and I went to look at the apartment. It was perfect for us. We put our deposit down and signed the lease and were ready to move in the next week. Back at home Lance was sleeping on the sofa which was the first in our relationship. He was removed, did not talk to me, he went out to his friends every night and the silence was relieving but also very unsettling. I was grateful for the lack of conflict. I felt I was going to be out soon and I feared any conflict leading up to it. On the night before I moved out he left and didn't return. He told me he'd be with his friends and don't wait up. I didn't have a chance to tell him I was moving, and I feared telling him because I didn't want him convincing me not to go. Years later I would find out in the one email correspondence we had that he hacked into my email and discovered I had signed the lease. He gave up on me. I felt he knew and he didn't want to ask why, what my plan was, or said he was finally willing to go to therapy.

My family whom I visited on that family trip that awakened me to a life filled with joy was visited by serendipity. And they were happy to help me move all of my stuff out, including pots and pans. This was it. This was really happening permanently. I can't believe it! And with the help of all my family. Those next few days were strange. I shared things that happened in our relationship with my family that I never had before. Lance never showed up, he gave me space to leave, which for a malignant narcissist was an event orchestrated by my guardian angel. It was as if the Divine left me no obstacles in the transition of the next right step in my life. I was still willing to work on our relationship at a distance through therapy. However, the second night in my new apartment, my sister revealed to me, a week earlier while we were in the midst of our final days, Lance had tried to seduce her into a hotel room. She was shocked, and confused and said "no". First I thought, why did you wait so long to tell me? Then I felt so hurt and betrayed. I knew he was scheming to get back at me and his plan failed. I had found my way out and was waiting for him to call to apologize and move forward into therapy. Then I received this news that showed me even if he did call, his words held no value and he didn't care about me or care to be in a giving relationship. He was only after what he benefited from our relationship under his control the whole time. In his mind he was always right and I was the one to apologize. I was so mad and this was the sign that he was not going to apologize and he meant to abuse me by cheating on me. I mustered up enough self-worth and believed in my heart to know I do not let cheaters back into my life. I had a long, unhealthy rope, but that was where I drew the line.

So I filed for divorce and that was the end of our relationship. We did not speak or have any contact except for two instances. One email a few years later that I initiated as I processed my healing. And a verbal assault text barrage as I publicly shared he sexually abused me. He berated me threatening to blackmail me with those photos and videos I mentioned earlier during our bedroom adventures. I joined the #metoo movement. Without mentioning his name or any reference to his identity, his guilty conscience couldn't handle it and his narcissistic ego stepped in to try and silence me.

Lance text- Don't accuse me as if I raped you! You Aziz Ansari'd me! We had consensual sex .

Raven - doesn't reply (now panicking and can't breathe)

Lance - Remember this night? (explicit photo attached of me giving a blow job and a video of us having sex on the sofa)

- This will be out if you continue .

- What is your address? Are you talking about me? or is it your new man. If he is hurting your kids I swear I will hurt him!

Raven - doesn't reply (now infuriated)

Lance- I will ruin your life

- What is your address? So I can send you a Cease and Desist."

Raven - doesn't reply (and called the cops, learning there is no offense to document, and is advised to block his number.)

So I finally woke up and blocked his number.

Of course, initially, my heart mourned and ached for what was in the past, and I was hurt deeply. I started going to therapy and I was diagnosed with PTSD and recovering from an emotional and sexual abusive relationship. It was nice to have the diagnosis to finally prove I wasn't going crazy. The PTSD would hit with a song on the radio, scent, local streets where I used to live, a memory. And I would have bouts of uncontrollable crying, feeling physically sick to my stomach, and waves in my body that felt like I was being stretched and contracted like a rubber band. My therapist told me it would take time to heal, and that I would.

One day when we had a session talking about my family of origin she said, "You are the one to break ancestral patterns." I didn't want that burden. I just wanted to feel better. But now that I am better I do understand what she meant. I see the patterns so clearly, with my parents, grandparents. The hard-headed ideas of old fashioned parenting have consequences on our relationships, with each other and with new ones formed. Cultivating an environment of controlling the beliefs of Catholicism and using guilt to motivate one's child to behave and make life choices aligned with the parents' beliefs is a formula for disaster, heartache, rebellion and emotional abuse. You witnessed this in my story in the first few chapters of this book. One's soul's journey and spiritual path should be allowed space for freedom. However our souls do choose our parents and bodies, with hardship included so I know I chose them for a reason and life lesson. That is being the one to break the ancestral patterns.

- **Haunted**

I awoke in the dead of night, with a sudden, uneasy feeling. I felt someone staring at me. I looked over to the source and it was a dark shadow figure standing in the corner near the window staring at me. I panicked, and turned the light on immediately knowing it was not a kind visit. The shadow disappeared. I pulled my Bible out, that I read at the time, and eased my nerves reading the soothing words. I then was able to fall asleep. This happened a couple times. I don't know why, who exactly it was, but my sense was it was the darkness that was attached to Lance that was pulling me into the vortex. It came to visit me, in its last ditch efforts to control me. I believe in ghosts, spiritual energetic entities good and bad. I believe there are entities beyond our existence that exist in the spirit realm. I had never believed it before that night, and since then I've done much research on this topic and have a solid belief that the dark shadow was not a person but an energy entity haunting me.

As I entered a new relationship soon after, I was haunted in an emotional form. I would compare my new boyfriend's actions against the only man I knew and accuse him of the same actions or motives of Lance. This man was far from the type of man Lance was, but I was so conditioned in that relationship to please him, relate in an unhealthy way that it took a toll on our relationship. We attended a relationship bootcamp event over three days. This bootcamp was so healing. It was where I faced Sally, my bully and released her. They create nicknames for all of us based on our introductions. I was so upset at myself for my mistake with Lance and I was scared I was echoing the patterns in our relationship, which I was. Their nickname for me was "Haunted."

- **PTSD**

American Psychology Association describes PTSD as a psychiatric disorder that can occur in people who have experienced or witnessed a traumatic event. PTSD is anxiety and flashbacks of a traumatic event that can be triggered by small or obvious things. PTSD can affect a person's ability to work and perform normal day's activities. It prevents one from relating to their family and friends. A person with PTSD can often seem disinterested or distant as they try not to think or feel in order to block out the painful memories. This disorder is characterized by three main types of symptoms, flashbacks and nightmares, emotional numbness, and avoidance of places, people and activities that are all reminders of trauma. And in my instance just meltdowns of releasing that energy and crying and feeling like my body is just sick and nauseous. I experienced feeling like I had a really high fever, but I didn't have a fever but my body had the exhaustion and waves of feeling my energy field was being stretched and let go like a rhythmic elastic band.

What is a trigger? A trigger is anything that starts the feeling of despair and anxiety. The trigger could be a person, place, thing, situation, a certain song, or a certain smell. Any of these may remind you of the trauma and it sets you on a PTSD symptom episode. Flashbacks come so sudden and your episode may appear in an instant. The flashback is an echo of a feeling before it even hits your brain. Sometimes triggers are obvious, for example a military veteran might be triggered by loud noises or it might be something subtle like for me seeing a round ball hanging on a car rear view mirror. The round ball triggered a memory of a scene I saw in a movie of a man with a gag ball in his mouth, tied up and about to be raped by another man. That memory then triggers the deep suppressed feeling of being used like a toy rather than caressed as a lover. It takes me back to the long nights, the porn, the alcohol, the anal, the hours of sex that dried and chafed me. And it makes me cry and feel nauseous and sick to my stomach. That negative energy is in my body and escaping through tears. If you shove it down and don't allow it out it is unhealthy. There are exercises, therapy and breathing techniques and just releasing it to the Universe is the best way to get through and diminish the episodes.

Even though sex was technically consensual, and it was with a partner that I was committed to, the alcohol and manipulative persuasion and punishment if I didn't do it, puts this into a category where this was sexual abuse. The PTSD was the reverberation of the low vibration that I allowed myself to be submitted to. On the outside, it looked very bright, healthy and consensual and there's no accusation there, but for me and my body and the things that I allowed myself to experience they reverberated as shudders in my core and they were not pleasurable as I faked it to be. I take responsibility for that poor judgment and know my motivation was to gain his love and acceptance perpetually. That was very draining and soul sucking. Just as I wrote that narcissists suck all of empaths' energy out.

The great news is that there is a solution to releasing and healing PTSD. By rewriting happy and healthy memories that rebuild over those wounded memories is one way and does take some time. This is not a quick fix and just when you think you have it all cleared and out of your system something will trigger it. Ten years after I first left I have very rare instances where I experience PTSD compared to my weekly occurrences, at the beginning. When I first left the relationship I was experiencing it maybe four times a week, that's almost every day I would also encounter nightmares and shadow figures.

There are three ways that you can work on releasing the PTSD energy that is stuck in you. This will enable you to not be triggered as often as you are when you first escape whatever traumatic situation you might have experienced.

1. EFT tapping - This is relieving and amazing. It taps all of your acupressure points while speaking in calm and love. Personally I did it right after relieving my PTSD through time and horse therapy, but it helped further release the stress of being a mother that I became. I wish I had discovered EFT tapping before when I was going through therapy. It's extremely effective and can even help you hold off your addictive urges. I personally have done it and it

is an alternative acupressure therapy treatment. It's used to restore balance to your disrupted energy. It has been an authorized treatment for War veterans with PTSD and it's demonstrated some benefits as to treat anxiety, depression, physical pain, and insomnia. Absolutely I can attest that it works. The method is so easy you can do it on your own at home. What you do is you tap on certain acupressure points and say certain phrases out loud. I have provided the exercise in the Emotional Toolbox at the end of his chapter. There is a typing cycle you go through three times and each time you finish a series of taps through all the acupressure points, you assess where your anxiety level is. You perform deep breathing in between and then you tap all of the acupressure points and say these phrases through again, then repeat. The first time through you say phrases acknowledging that you are stressed and you have anxiety. The second time through, you question "what's the worst that can happen?" And then the third time through you affirm that you are calm, you are cool and you are not stressed. It is an exercise that is calming your nervous system down and taking it out of the fight or flight mode, which is what PTSD is doing, due to the trigger. All those emotions then can be erased.

2. The second one is to get in touch with nature. Water, nature and animal therapy is an alternative that really helped me during the time of my healing and transition from out of my old life to my new life. In the midst of leaving my Savior, rock and abuser I also decided he didn't control my choice about staying in a job I grew to hate. I quit my job shortly after I left Lance. I loved horses ever since I could remember, and I was gifted a horse during the last year of my marriage. The horse was a gift from my

childhood trainer whom I rode and trained with as a child. I competed in Hunter/Jumper and dressage. And on the most horrible of nights I would drive in the middle of the night and go visit my horse at the barn while everyone was asleep. I would take him out to graze and lean on him and cry on him. He was so patient and majestic. At the end of my marriage and career in Corporate sales, I thought I would start a horse teaching business. With all my experience I didn't believe it would be that hard. It was so enjoyable and extremely relaxing at the same time the business was extremely hard on my body and there were some dramatic moments with panicking horses on trail.

I would not recommend starting a horse business, but find a therapeutic riding center or a therapy dog. The great thing about equine or dogs is you can interact with them in nature. Another benefit to equine therapy is the left and right swaying allows your body to calm down as if you were in your mothers womb again and feel the soothing left, right sensation. There have been studies proving that the left and right movement in your body including your eyes tracking an object going left and right soothes the nerves. You would receive the same benefits if you went walking, you're getting that left, right motion soothing your nervous system dispelling the PTSD. Experiencing homeostasis is a feeling that is extremely soothing. A float tank or floating in a bath would also be very soothing. If you are nervous about getting up on a horse, riding doesn't even need to happen. Just being in the presence of that giant majestic horse is therapy in itself. Standing and feeling their energy and their presence and their magical energy. They hold a sacred space for you to talk, feel, and heal. Find a therapy center near you that includes horses or dogs. Dogs give you an unconditional love and playfulness that cuts through your pain and heartache. You can cuddle with them, just petting them transfers their positive and healing energy. Adopting a pet is another option if you are up for the task of taking care of a permanent fur toddler. The benefit of being able to walk them, get outside in nature and spending time cuddling them is very healing.

3. The third is EMDR Therapy. Which is all about left, right, left, right movement in the brain. EMDR is a therapy that helps you connect with a traumatic experience and rewrite and reconnect it with new information. It is effective, yet also time consuming; it is a long process. In my interview with Jessica Mroz, she talked extensively about EMDR. She did it herself for her therapy and it was extremely helpful for her. She said it was a long road and it was really traumatic as she had to revisit the distressing thoughts and emotions in order to rewrite them but now the events were excised from her psyche and rewritten, as a result her PTSD was alleviated. It aids in releasing that energy that is stuck in your body and your body energy in trauma and mind.

We can't deal with something if we can't even acknowledge it. First step is getting you safe. You focus on how you feel in each part of your body. Before you do the heavy duty work, you need a support system, strategies, and cannot do it alone. ... So with PTSD you go back to that emotional state that you were in when the trauma happened, however you don't have an awareness of that until you start getting into the work. EMDR they track your eye movements right and left with finder or light, or tap left and right. It activates both sides of the brain as if you are dreaming with rapid eye movement. When we are traumatized, the accelerator and brakes occur at the same time and you lose consciousness. As a child or adult you don't fight back and shut down for self protection like a possum playing dead.... The reason why right left works, when that circuit breaker shuts down. The right side of the brain is more visual and the left side, the logical shuts down. So there is no narrative, no time. There is no sense of time so the trauma keeps living in your body as if it never ended. ...And it may lay dormant for a long time and something triggers it. The memories are fragmented so it brings confusion and the emotion of that stamp in time. ... In EMDR you revisit the initial memory, and then explain what happened in your body, and then as your eyes track back and forth you then associate what had happened with other events in your life that your brain associated together. ...And having the right and left brain online at the same time by moving the eyes, now you've integrated the memory back into the brain in a way that it knows it is over. ... You feel the emotions that you didn't allow yourself to feel. ... Your body is allowed to feel the grief or sadness you've never allowed yourself to feel. ... Some sessions reach a resolution or it might be continued to the next session.

EMDR is very powerful, however there are multiple ways to heal and remove the stuck trauma from your body and these are the three most effective methods.

What I found that helped me continue to heal deeper were meditations. Meditations are also a tool for rewriting negative patterns and energy. The Inner Child is the single most powerful meditation for healing of the past and taking care of yourself. That guided meditation is in the Emotional Toolbox at the end of Chapter 4 and on the Raven Scott Show YouTube Channel, in the Meditation Playlist.

Treasures I lost: Peace of Mind

Human Design Element:
All of my centers and chakras and nervous system out of balance. Read more about Human Design in Chapter 12.

Learn how to practice EFT tapping on the next page.

Dive Deeper into this topic in S3 Episode 55:Emotional Burnout Antidote from Toxic people & Narcissist Relationships with Anne Berube on the Empath & Narcissist Podcast.

-   EFT TAPPING

I recommend doing it daily for 28 days to form a habit. That's how I started. I did it for a whole month, every day, at the beginning of my day. I wanted to bring my anxiety down so that I would not yell at my children, period. Part of the healing process is our nervous system is deregulated and we yell and take it out on our loved ones. And my anxiety was probably at 9 out of 10. I was up there; everything was bottled inside my throat chakra was closed. I was holding it all in. I fell into the trap of thinking I had to do everything on my own and not ask for help. Comparing myself to society says we have to do or be perfect like Pinterest or social media perfect. So bringing my anxiety down from a 9 down to 7, then 5. Halfway through the month I was able to get it down to a 3, and by the time I was done on day 30 I was at a 0.

You can practice on the Raven Scott Show YouTube channel. "How to Stop Anxiety Attacks: EFT Tapping Practice." You can access the full Meditation library in the Meditation Playlist.

Transcript is here:

Stress Buster Meditation

This EFT tapping therapy is extremely effective if you concentrate and lean into feeling and talking your way through your anxiety while honoring your acupressure points and tapping them. Try practicing this every morning for two weeks, if you feel it's helping then extend your practice to two more weeks until it becomes a habit and these positive phrases become rooted in your subconscious. And when events arise they will not be as stressful because you know everything will be OK.

First step is to take a deep breath and observe what level your anxiety is at. From 0-10. 0 being none , and 10 being the highest. Then start by tapping each point and stating the phrases following the letter A.

After you've gone through all the letter A phrases while tapping, stop and take a deep breath and rate your stress level again. Observe, has it gone down, up? Or remained the same. Any is ok. Then Go through the tapping stating phrases following the letter B. Repeat breathing and rate of stress level 0-10, and do the last round of tapping stating phrases following after the letter C. Once finished take a deep breath and assess where your stress level is at. Be thankful and absorb the positive energy and say a prayer to your higher self, the Universe or God.

Note: You can customize what the phrase says based on what you are feeling or worrying about at the moment.

A good time to do this exercise is in the morning, however you can do it at any time depending on how you feel. The goal is to carry on with your day knowing the Universe has you and don't worry because thinking about the worry makes it worse. Surrender your worry and tap it away to enjoy life as stress free as you desire.

EFT Tapping
Breathe. Rate 0-10 stress before each round.
- Tap karate chop part of hand rhythmically
  A. Even though I'm anxious and upset, I deeply and completely love and accept myself.
  B. Even though I'm anxious, I deeply and completely love and accept myself.
  C. Even though I am anxious, I choose to completely love and accept myself.
- Tapping eyebrow point (inside nearest nose)
  A. I'm so upset (repeat saying as many times that feels good ie 3-5 times)

    B. This upset, stress, and worry is so uncomfortable

    C. I'm calm, confident, and relaxed

- Tapping Out side of eye

    A. What if the worst happens

    B. I know this situation isn't going to last forever

    C. I choose to know everything is going to be ok

- Tapping under the eye

    A. What if the worst happens

    B. I know this situation isn't going to last forever

    C. I choose to see this moment as safe

- Tap[2]ping under the nose

    A. What will I do, how will I handle it

    B. Maybe I just need to take a break and vent

    C. I choose to be calm, confident and relaxed

- Tapping chin

    A. It's all up to me and I'm feeling overwhelmed now

    B. Maybe I just need to get relief from all things in life

    C. Calming down now, relaxing my body

- Tapping collarbone

    A. I wish I could calm down

    B. This too shall pass

    C. Feels good to take a break feeling calm and relaxed

- Tapping under arm below armpit

    A. I'm so worried and I'm anxious

    B. I know I can calm down and I welcome the shift

    C. Calm, confident and relaxed

- Tapping top of head

    A. I want to push this away but I can't

    B. I honor my experience and accept my situation completely

C. I choose to accept myself and my situation completely. Everything is going to be ok.

- REMOVING DARK ENERGY

Anger letter and burn exercise

This is a powerful tool to release the hate, the sadness, and disappointment that you are unable to freely express to that person. Or maybe you had to flee, break contact and block them from your life. This is a freeing way to gain closure. Write the letter, write it all out, tears included. When you are finished writing all the sadness, hurt and negativity into your letter. At the end of the letter thank your offender for whatever lesson you learned. And then *safely* burn the letter in a stainless steel pot clear of anything it can set fire on as the flame will reach 12" above the top of the pot's rim. After you safely burn this letter and transmute and release the energy up to the Source. Shower immediately or as soon as possible after to cleanse away the energy with the magical healing powers of water.

Forgiveness letter

On a different date, write a letter of forgiveness to your offender. If you are unable to find forgiveness write the letter to your offender's inner child. Imagine them at age seven and release your resentment and forgive them and thank them for the life lesson presented to you through this hardship. Your forgiveness will not relinquish their souls journey and karma of any lessons they will learn or receive in this life or another. It is not stating to the Universe they didn't do wrong, however holding in unforgiveness is just as if you drank poison wishing the other person to die. Let Karma run its course and have peace to know they will answer for their ill treatment in the after life. When you are finished with this letter burn it safely, transmuting and releasing the energy up to Source. Shower immediately or as soon as possible after to cleanse away the energy with the magical healing powers of water.

8. SUBTLE SIGNS OF COVERT NARCISSISM

Breaking The Generational Curse

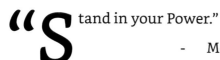"**S**tand in your Power."

- Message from my Healed Ancestor.

- **Judgements**

This journey as an empath of falling into a narcissists trap is painful enough as an isolated incident. But as I healed and uncovered the "why" I fell prey to Lance's schemes, I entered a new realm of pain, hurt and unhealthy patterns through rekindling my relationship with my family. It became apparently clear I was not only codependent on Lance, but I was codependent on my parents, siblings, aunt, and friends. The journey of finding my power took me back to the beginning of this soul's journey. I realized I was making decisions and living for approval of everyone trying to fit into their box they admired. I'll share some insidious phrases to paint the picture of the environment that made me tread so carefully on eggshells as a child; making the people pleasing lifestyle normalized.

"We are not Mormon!" Even though there is a whole lineage of

Mormon's documented, that is his ancestry, hidden from me until I was an adult.

"I am not from apes or ooze!" My father shutting down conversations about science and evolution.

"The Bible says 'you shall not be unequally yoked.' " When I wanted to be in a relationship with a Christian African American boy who's mother was white.

"Because I sad so!" the end of all discussions when I asked why a rule was in place.

"You must repent or you will go to hell." I heard every week at church

"That's just disgusting!" When gay love was on TV or on the news.

The judgements talked behind others backs, loved ones backs and to their face, and laws passed to control their bodies, is all a result of toxic covert/ noble narcissism.

> *"Judge not, that ye be not judged." from their own Bible*
> *Matthew 7:1*

The irony is their intense resistence to inclusivity has forced them to reconcile with these judgements with both daughters having sex before marriage, both divorced, one (myself) in an interracial marriage, and a granddaughter in the LGBTQ community. These circumstances are evidence their firm beliefs were built on a foundation of sand.

This is my ancestral patterns I strive to break and I know this is also the majority of our ancestral patterns as well. With 80% and more in a belief structure that holds ancient judgements on how a person must act and be that is so black and white. I strive to break the fixed ideas from my conditioning and strive to love each person because of their uniqueness. I intend to allow the ebb and flow with the lessons life and my children bring into our lives. I strive for neutrality, standing in my authority and self sovereignty, and being open to be used by Source for the greater good.

Growing up I felt the pressure to be perfect and not judged. And that urged me to strive to monitor my self worth on how polite I was, how selfless I should be, how homogenous I should be, and how straight and narrow my spiritual path must take. In my personal experience this left me with no freedom in my religious or spiritual journey. The only way it seemed to exist was within the fold, or completely out of the good graces of my family. The unspoken and spoken judgement is so toxic like poison in the air. I would breathe in that a good Catholic marries another Catholic. And the unspoken I would breathe in was a good white girl should marry a devout white male. Same sex marriages was outwardly spoken against as "disgusting". And in the words of my grandmother, "If you are not taking your children to church, you might as well take them straight to hell." This poison .... Affected me in ways that I didn't have a safe space to process new ideas and possibilities in life. My true soul's discovery was not safe to share with my family. I found safety in my new Savior and Narcissist. Which as you've read was not healthy or a happy outcome for me. This mindset of one way or hell is a poison that was created to control the subjects of those in power all the way back in Medieval times. I intend to keep this poison out of my home and not breathe this to my children.

From the moment I discovered the beautiful life growing inside me was a girl, I vowed to myself I would work ten times harder to heal the wounds, break ancestral patterns, and improve my emotional intelligence beyond my wildest imagination. This sexual abuse relationship was just the struggle my soul knew I needed to fast track my evolution and learning on this Earth. I didn't know how, I just believed that Source would direct me on the right path.

I believe children are not to be controlled or lorded over, they are souls here to be guided. I don't want to be a guide who holds restrictive expectations and feels disappointment when that child doesn't live up to my expectation. I want to be a parent who discovers and explores the new elements that my child discovers about themselves and celebrates with them. I love Human Design and I love to learn the road map and characteristics of my child's soul's purpose. But more importantly I love discovering what lights them up.

-   **Boxes**

As humans on this Earth, we love putting each other in boxes and categories. This brings us order and understanding to things. But the problem is when such unique and complex souls are organized in such a way, some of the souls feel suffocated and like imposters residing in this box society puts them in. We have a box for male, female, mom, dad, professional, Lesbian, Gay, Bisexual, Transgendered and more. I hate the boxes because most of us souls would fit in multiple boxes at once. But culture doesn't like one person being in more than one box. What if the boxes were knocked down? Only then would all of us, just like Lego pieces, were free to mix and build together to create masterpieces. This is another reason I love Human Design. It shows us what type of puzzle piece we uniquely are.

Recently my six year old daughter wanted to cut her hair. Her style is "cool" not "cute" she tells me. She has shopped in the boys clothing section for as long as she could walk and she loves any sport she tries. She also exudes the feminine side always being the patient loving big sister and babysitter at all our playdates and playing with baby dolls, and art, and all the colors of the rainbow. One day she asked for a haircut like a certain boy in a show. I have to admit, I had to rewrite my ancestral pattern and subdue the squirms I was feeling. My fears of judgements made me uncomfortable with her cutting her beautiful, curly hair away to be spiked and buzzed. I searched Pinterest for girls' hairstyles that were edgy. I found multiple pictures of women rocking the buzz cut and looked feminine and powerful which soothed my fears. Regardless of how I felt, this is what she wanted. And if I had convinced her or told her this hairstyle is for boys not girls, she would've felt dismissed and invalidated. She would have felt unseen, unheard, and judged for wanting to look a certain way. In her mind this is how she feels most comfortable in her skin. After six years of self improvement and rewriting my mirror neurons, I quickly erased the fears in my head and reminded myself that this was an amazing discovery. She rocks playing with Barbies, can't wait to grow up and be a nurturing mother *and* rocks her sporty side. After I finished transforming her hair style from a cutie curly haired "girl" into a cool buzz "boy" look, she beamed ear to ear. She had a glow and shine about her that showed me she had stepped into her own skin. The shock of the physical transformation made my parents mute. Unapproving and full of fears she will be "transgender". They didn't have to say anything, the message was loud and clear. But I am confident in her journey and my parenting. I did not let it bother me for too long. On the other hand my adult niece applauded and encouraged me for breaking gender barriers and allowing her the freedom to look as she wished. I appreciated the praise, however what mattered the most to me was that her soul felt seen, heard and loved. I believed that we both discovered something about her soul that will help challenge our view of the judgements and boxes we put each other in. That day I celebrated how much I had transformed in my emotional intelligence.

- **Re-writing Mirror neurons**

Mirror Neurons are the neurons that fire off in your brain and teach you how to do something by observing. These start developing during the infantile stage. You observe your parents move a certain way, say things a certain way, pick up utensils, talk about themselves, and more! Then as you repeat that motion, your brain locks in and imprints that style of being and doing. The positive is we can teach our young and lead by example. The negative is they pick up all our bad habits along with the good skills. For myself I recognized I had such a low self image about myself. I recalled back as far as I could go in my memories. It was a well known fact that my mother did not have a healthy body image. She was cautious about her weight and it was something she struggled with in my youth. I realized I picked up on her body image issues and not feeling pretty enough, skinny enough to meet society's standards. Again humans have a box labeled skinny waist women and buxom women. And the skinny waist box is raised up on a pedestal to be unattainably aspired to. I subconsciously would say the same thing that I was not pretty, and felt I truly wasn't compared to my friends. I could also blame society, commercials, magazines, media and movies for casting the same type of woman in their roles. As children, what we watch is also logged into our brain, that is how we must act. And what is modeled is locked into our psyche over what is taught to us through language. My father would continually compliment me and tell me I was beautiful. I did not believe him, every time I would say "You are just saying that because you are my dad."

Once I became aware of what mirror neurons were I had the power to recognize them and then rewrite them. Have you ever caught yourself sounding exactly like your parents? There is an insurance commercial that jokes about it. These are the mirror neurons recurring and you saying or acting as your parent. If this element of your parents you resent, felt as a child were hurt by, more than likely you are hurting your child with it as well. The good news is you can stop it. You can reprogram yourself. The first step is recognizing it. The moment you catch yourself, you have the chance to rewrite it. It will take a succession of times to correct and reprogram but each time you will strengthen your muscles in the direction you choose.

For example, I was able to rewrite my self image story for myself. Anytime I started to show disgust with my big butt, or my face or my nose. I would stop mid sentence and turn the sentence around. "Ugh I hate how - I mean I love how my nose is uniquely designed just for my face. I am so grateful it is symmetrical and clear of obstructions so I may breathe in oxygen freely."

The mirror work exercise at the end of this chapter will help start to reprogram your self esteem, body image, and behaviors.

Another distinct time I remember catching myself and rewriting the narrative was when my youngest toddler was upset and crying in the car. With my open Solar Plexus and her tone just sends my anxiety from 0 to 100. I caught myself telling her one day. "Stop, just stop, I need peace and quiet." I immediately felt guilty, stupid and the echo of being told to be quiet when I was younger shattered my bones. In my next breath I said. "No scratch that. I'm sorry. You may cry all you need to get out whatever you're feeling out. Get it all out. That's it." This was my first lesson in holding space for my child who has constant waves of highs and lows and is just a daily occurrence, multiple times a day when she is feeling low. Her Solar Plexus is defined. And she was a toddler, that's just what they do. I will explain more about Human Design in Chapter 12.

You may rewrite your mirror neurons for your new business venture, your relationship with money, your relationship with your partner, your relationship with food, and addictions. It takes time and effort, but the reward will be so sweet. I have transformed so much in the last six years. I have love and confidence for myself I have never had in my whole life. Now when I walk by the mirror I don't see the ugly I used to see. I just see me, beautiful, strong, and compassionate.

- **Standing in your Power**

One day you will be ready to break the patterns in your relationship with your parent(s). You will wake up to the fact that your parents' manipulative persuading for you to step in line with the rules of the house may still continue to repeat in your adult life with them today. These patterns are formed and are not going to break unless you react differently to them. It won't show up as a tool to get you to be obedient but it will show up as a tool for you to act to go along with their plan, or it may be guilt over how you raise your children. These patterns are not invented by your parents, these patterns have been passed down generation after generation. They don't mean to be hurtful, it is out of their subconscious survival tactics that these unhealthy interactions come about. We all have our inner child that is wounded and in need of healing, even our parents. And the day will come when you start to break just one of these patterns. It will be uncomfortable for all parties. But in order for you to stand in your power and change the behavior that is passed to your children that is a small price to pay.

I remember my four year old toddler, whom some may label as sensitive, was visiting with my parents at our home. She had a special stack of books that she didn't let anyone touch. Since the day I knew I was chosen to guide two girls I have been a huge advocate of consent. I always taught them and their friends the option of a high five or hug at greetings. This I also taught them with adults, even family members and grandparents. This consent included respecting their requests in not touching their special items. And my husband and I respected her request, especially since she was so adamant. I knew it was important for her development to have some control and sovereignty. She shared this request to my father and he asked "Oh like this?" while touching them. She was offended and immediately stormed off to her room and shut the door crying. At that moment my inner child was in fight or flight mode as well. He was baffled at how she got so upset, he said he was just joking. At first I tried to keep the peace and say, "It's ok, give her time and she will come out." I went to her bedroom. She had locked the door so I tried to coax her out. She would not open the door. So I assured her I was here when she was ready to talk. I went back down to the living room. He started to feel bad and he went to the door to apologize to her. She yelled out "No. I am not coming out." He instantly became mad and I was suddenly faced with defending my daughter or keeping the peace and making him right and throwing my daughter in a position where she was chastised for her behavior. The all too familiar gut drop feeling arrived in the pit of my stomach. He huffed "Is this appropriate behavior for a four year old?" I took a deep pause and tried to calm my trembling nerves. I replied "Yes, actually it is. You crossed her boundary she drew, she is upset and she will need time to get her feelings out and trust again." He walked away and eventually she opened her door and came out to me and was able to accept his apology in the safety of my arms. That day I graduated from an obedient daughter, to a warrior mother.

- **Healed Ancestor**

This reprogramming is exactly how you will break the ancestral patterns that are unhealthy in your family. Believe it or not, there once was a healed ancestor in your lineage. I will walk you through a guided Healed Ancestor Meditation at the end of this chapter, and you will be shocked at whom yours is.

When I first performed this I had no idea I was going to meet a Native American Cherokee woman. She appeared to be an elder or shaman. I had no information in any of my research that we had Cherokee in our family. Her family line is a mystery to us. The paperwork stops at her mother. Her father died in a car fire when she was eight. The next day I was on my weekly call to my grandmother. We started talking about her father and her life back in South Carolina. She spoke of her grandfather, her father's father. He ran the local general store and when he passed he passed on a decent amount of money to her and her brother. She said that is how we were able to make our start in their first home purchase. I asked do you know anything about his family? She answered that she remembered that her father and his family came from the Cherokee Indians in Oklahoma. My jaw dropped. "What?" I said. "Does anyone have any papers?" She answered she would have to ask her cousin. I was shocked. Just the day before I was confused about why a Cherokee woman would come to me in my healed ancestor meditation. This is an illustration that you will be shocked when you lean in and trust Divine's guidance.

- **Written in the Stars**

As I dive deeper in interpreting my Natal Astrology chart. I find I have My North Node in Gemini and my 10th House. The North Node is a representative of Karma, a nod to our spiritual growth. Gemini is the zodiac full of logic, information, and communication. And the 10th House is where one's public reputation and career lie. My soul wants to be responsible for my life. In the past, this life and past life, I stepped back from the opportunity to fight for my goals in order to please my family. I also have Uranus, the planet of rebellion in my 4th house that holds family and parental energies. In my past life regression I know I ran away from home at 21 to search after my soul's purpose and away from family duties. In this life I pleased my parents until I was 18 and my soul wanted to rebel and discover the truth and explore my goals and opportunities. My soul wants to understand my emotional response and let go of patterns that do not serve me anymore. After everytime I interact with my family and have emotional reactions I am psycho analyzing it for days. That also is a sign that I have been gaslighted by my family.

My soul longs to be independent and free. In writing this book I believe that is a manifestation of that very desire. I desire to replace my insecurities with plans. South Node in the 4th house, of family and parents I took care of others needs at my expense. I was obedient, I didn't rock the rules and ideas that my parents held on to so tightly in order that I wouldn't cause more heartache in the wake of my sister's leaving. But as a mother and leader of my own household, I needed to focus on myself more and self care. I have been doing that the past six years and it has served me well and I have grown and matured with leaps and bounds. The goal is to set healthy emotional boundaries so I may be a guide to my children rather than control them. In the other realm one may experience a haunting of a ghost versus a gentle loving visit from an ancestor or spirit guide. I desire to be their ancestor guiding them, not an overbearing and controlling parent that haunts them emotionally when I interact with them. It is my role and responsibility in this life to break the pattern of emotional guilt, emotional judgement, and emotional control. Setting emotional healthy boundaries and keeping the fear and judgement out of our home allows me to set the stage for that alchemy to transpire. This is possible for you as well, if you desire.

Treasure I found: Clarity

Human Design element at play:
My open will center healing and putting up a screen to filter out what is my ideas and agenda and what is not.

Dive Deeper into this topic in S3 Episode 32: The Bizarre Truth Behind Trauma Bonding in Relationships and Ancestral Healing on the Empath & Narcissist Podcast.

-   MIRROR WORK PART 2

Rewrite toxic mirror neurons

First write down your character flaws and physical attributes you dislike.

Then for each of those you are going to reverse the narrative and belief. Write an affirmation about these "flaws".

Then create a reminder on your phone with this affirmation . Or create post cards and place them up on your mirror. Or create a graphic and make it your lock screen wallpaper.

Stand in front of the mirror and look into your eyes and say these affirmations.

Start with one for 28 days. and then once you truly believe this affirmation (it more than likely will take longer than 28 days btw) stop that affirmation and move to the next affirmation, reciting it into the mirror, talking into your soul.

I'm not going to lie, this is going to be one of the hardest things to do. The Ego wants to hold onto the negative thoughts to protect you. But these narratives are holding you back, keeping you a victim and in this pain cycle.

Once you embrace your flaws as perfection you will transform and thrive.

-   CONNECT WITH YOUR HEALED ANCESTOR

1. Healed Ancestor Journaling

- o   Write out all you know of your Father's line. The negative patterns, things you wished were healed, and the positive traits they passed on.
- o   Write out all you know of your Mother's line. The negative patterns, things you wished were healed, and the positive traits they passed on.

2. Healed Ancestor Meditation

You can practice this on the Raven Scott Show YouTube channel. And access the whole library in the Meditation Playlist.

Transcript:

Find a comfortable place to sit in a quiet space that is private. Close your eyes. Elongate your spine nice, tall or long. Take a deep breath in and a deep breathe out. Place your left hand on your heart and your right hand on your belly. Take a deep breath in again and feel the rise of your belly and chest and out through mouth, ha. Take a deep breathe in and out. Ha. …Now breathe nice and easy now and steady. Relaxed breathing.

Envision a root or roots growing from your tail bone or spine down into the surface you are on. See them root and continue to move deep into the layers of the Earth. Down, down, down, and reaching the Earth's mantle. They grab hold of a glowing crystal in the magma. The light of this crystal shines bright and starts to illuminate your roots. The light travels slowly back up the roots towards your body. Slowly through the Earth's layers, through the rocks, sediment, layers, dirt, foundation, floor and into your roots attached to your body. The white light travels up through your spine and out the top of your head and golden and white sparkling light pours over your head, and rains over your body. As you envision this light showering you, repeat this invocation with me.

" Supreme Infinity, Divine Father Sky, Divine Mother Earth, Avatars, Ascended Masters, Archangels, Holy Angels, Spirit Guides, Healed Ancestors, and all my Teachers (name any specifically by name). Only entities and energies for my highest good are allowed in this space. And with the help of my Higher Self, I invoke for the Divine Light, Divine Love, and Divine Power. Bless me abundantly with Wisdom, Strength, Courage to find power, balance, equanimity, alignment, and the deepest healing on all levels of all my energy bodies.

In my deepest soul's heart in full faith, Thank you. So Be It, and So It Is."

Now envision yourself in a safe space. It could be a forest, a field, a church, your home, anywhere that is safe to you. You start to see your ancestors as light beams starting to come from afar closer and closer. They encircle you and you feel their love and warmth. You may see faces, you may not. You may start to see human form shaping out of the light. Feel their safety encircling you and caring for you.

After a bit of time, ask your healed ancestor to step forward. Wait for yourself to feel or see your healed ancestor step forward. They have a message for you. First sit/stand in their love. What do you look like? What do you feel? What is their clothing? What is their culture? What is their name? Wait for the answers to come.

Now ask them. "What do you need to tell me?" Wait for the answer through feeling, telepathy, hearing, or knowing.

Thank your healed ancestor for stepping forward. Thank them for the message they brought you today. Invite them to stay with you and come and go as they please.

When you are ready, thank Source, Divine Father Sky, Divine Mother Earth, Stellar Centers, Maha Avatars, Ascended Masters, Archangels, Holy Angels, Spirit Guides, Healed Ancestors, and all your teachers.

I am you, we are one, all is well. Thank you. Namaste.

Slowly wiggle your toes, and fingers. Start to breathe in deep breaths again to bring your soul back to your Earthly body. Slowly blink your eyes open. Write down in your journal anything and everything you want to note about your experience.

You may recite this breaking chords prayer for additional clearing.

- Breaking chords prayer :

I acknowledge the ties that bind to my (fill in the blank mother / father) and their insecurities. I see those chords unraveling and severed.

I acknowledge the ties that bind to my (fill in the blank mother / father) and their anger. I see those chords unraveling and severed.

I acknowledge the ties that bind to my (fill in the blank mother / father) and their abandonment. I see those chords unraveling and severed.

I acknowledge the ties that bind to my (fill in the blank mother / father) and their weakness. I see those chords unraveling and severed.

I acknowledge the ties that bind to my (fill in the blank mother / father) and their mute voice against bullies. I see those chords unraveling and severed.

I acknowledge the ties that bind to my (fill in the blank mother / father) and their God-like judgements. I see those chords unraveling and severed.

I acknowledge the ties that bind to my (fill in the blank mother / father) and their serving others at my expense. I see those chords unraveling and severed.

I acknowledge the ties that bind to my (fill in the blank mother / father) and their work-aholic state. I see those chords unraveling and severed.

The chords are not severed, may I work to heal, understand and learn the purpose of this life's lessons. Bless this life with wisdom, strength and courage, so my soul may be in alignment, balance and harmony. Thank you in full faith. Through all time and space, Sky and Earth, so be it, and so it is.

9. THE TRUTH ABOUT NARCISSISTS

How to Heal from them

"Do not dwell in the past, do not dream of the future, concentrate the mind on the present moment."

- Buddha

- Heal With Love

For all the lessons learned and mistakes made in my past, it does not allow me to move forward if I continue to beat myself up about it. The same applies to you. Whatever your situation is or was, you are thankful for the karmic lesson, focus on your mental health today, and strive for balance and enlightenment to reside in your life now. You deserve forgiveness and grace just as much as your offender. Sometimes we allow ourselves to forgive others, but we build an armor to protect ourselves and never forgive ourselves for the choices we made. Focusing on the knowledge that we have multiple lives to learn these lessons over has given me great perspective. Even if you are not sure if we have multiple lives, you can look at your life as if you were on your deathbed, and in this one life, in the overarching picture, ask yourself; did that mistake teach you a spiritual lesson? The answer is always yes. So let yourself have grace, know you were destined to make that mistake and it was well orchestrated by your soul in order to achieve one step closer to enlightenment.

In this human existence and current 21st century culture, every influence is urging us to be perfect. With retailers modeling certain body types, people posting perfect moments on Instagram, and our parents pushing us to work hard, get good grades and have a solid career. We are influenced to believe what our family believes in all to be "perfect" under the guise of wanting us to have a happy and easy life. This is a delusion a parent desires for their precious baby as they grow in this world. It is not our Karmic path to have an easy life. So making mistakes and experiencing life as our soul is destined to is part of this beautiful life's process. I'd dare say if life is smooth sailing with no hiccups, you are asleep to your soul's path in learning lessons here on Earth school. I also wager, if you are reading this book your life hasn't been an easy one. Therefore, let go of the guilt and shame over your poor choice and mistakes.

What if your codependency or bad relationships was what your soul needed? I personally believe my comfort and safety with Lance that I felt at first was the environment I needed to have my horizons expanded. My knowledge of the world was narrow and naive, I didn't know anything about astronomy or evolution. I was a zombie and deeply conditioned. And even though I felt I could not live without him, it was a sort of jolt into a new direction onto a new path that was more awakened, and expanded to the potential truths I would eventually learn. It woke me up out of the cult-like religion, I was entrenched in, and freed me of my closed minded philosophies. Regretfully, I made mistakes against my better judgement and allowed him to take my power away from me. Those mistakes hurt many people, friends, my parents, my aunt, my cousin/sisters, my sister, and even my nieces. The challenge was to truly awaken from this human slumber, find the signs and unlatch myself from him. I was able to remove the hold, or hypnosis he had on me. I was able to find freedom and light in this new higher path full of Spirit guides, enlightenment, and my soulmate.

-   Soulmates

Even though I had a strong connection to Lance and a false sense that he was my soulmate, I believe he was just a karmic friend. Even with all the hurt he caused and heartache and control, I believe he is a young soul, who was so broken and on a tumultuous path himself. It was the human pleasures and my worship of status that confused me and allowed for him to have a hold on me. The narcissists expert song and dance of love bombing, then neglect and shaming was a perpetual cycle my deep empathic being thought I could fix. The feelings we have in our human bodies can be confusing to our soul's needs. Just as with my constant struggle to leave and move out, going and then returning, my soul had moments of clarity to move on, but my human emotions and body were so tethered to his. In the spiritual world there are elements called energetic chords, and trackers. I truly believe he had an evil entity that took over his goodness, and it chorded me in the dark vortex as well. At the end of our relationship, I could see and sense the tracker and chord. I saw the dark mist, I saw the dark vortex that I was being pulled into. I knew I was awake then and had to get out.

A soulmate is like an old sweater. They feel comfortable, familiar, and like home. They are not all about the flash and appearances. It is not the obsessive crush type love. Those are like a firecracker, and the joy fizzles fast. Soulmate love is a low burning fire that lasts all night. It's a beautiful soulful comfortable spark of love that connects you deep in an unexplainable kind of way. They love you at your most unpresentable moments, give you space, and at the same time respect your choices. Don't commit or marry the "best sex of your life guy." That will just bring you drama and heartache. Go with the old trustworthy true love.

Shortly after I left and started my new horse business, I received an email from a potential new client. They had three horses and wanted to learn how to jump. Because of the gender neutral name I assumed it was a middle aged woman. At the same time they were expecting to meet a middle aged woman because I exaggerated my years of horse training experience and signed off my emails with "Namaste". The day we met I had not showered, put on any makeup, and was dressed in grubby horse clothes. When we met it was so shocking to both of us. They were a "he" and I was a "young attractive woman." Our expectations were far from what the reality was and at the same time we both had a comfortable familiarity about us. It felt so congenial as if we had known each other forever. I felt completely at ease in *his* presence. It felt like when you meet up with a long lost friend and you start off where you left as if no time had passed. In the span of thirty hours from when we met, we spoke for many hours on the phone, went on a date and kissed. It may appear on the outside I was desperately lonely, however I was content with my new roommate and single life. It was because my vibration was high and aligned with my freedom and higher self that I attracted what the Universe wanted for me. Our first kiss felt like all memories and senses came back flooding back in an otherworldly magic. You know as they depicted it in the movies where the camera spins around the couple and the whole world blurs? I had experienced intense love emotions before from Lance many times over, however this felt cosmic. This felt different, this felt like coming home. And over time he proved his intentions were true and he gave me the unleashed freedom to explore who I was, my career, my healing path, and my spiritual journey. He was and still is my solid tree rooted deep in the ground amongst my storms and hurricanes of emotions, dramas, and discoveries. Confident in himself, he went along with me when I wanted to go back to the church, then leave. I have the freedom to do my meditations, go to Buddhist temples, go to yoga, spiritual retreats, and tell him all my "woo woo ideas" with maybe some questions yet without judgements. I know I've lucked out in finding my soulmate so soon after. I was aware and knew the most common occurrence is for an abused woman or man to fall into another abusive relationship because of the subconscious patterns. However I also want to attribute the fact that I was going to therapy during that time and I was aware and working on rewriting my subconscious patterns. I had an entire session with my therapist discussing if moving forward in marriage was aligned with my highest good and it wasn't a repeat of my past.

I want you to know you can find your soulmate. I believe we have many soulmates that are here in this life from our familiar Soul pod. To find your true love and soulmate, there are three things you can do.

1. You must believe they exist and that good men exist.
2. You must believe you are worthy of love and connection with your soul mate.
3. You must not work so hard to book dates, call men and chase them. Set your love intentions and wait for the Universe to bring your paths together.

-   Growth Mindset

How we respond to stress creates chemicals in our body of disease. Kindness and strength creates ease in our body. Shame shuts down our learning part of the brain and disables us to problem solve. This is why it is such a powerful tool used by the narcissist. If they can make you feel guilty they have power over your brain. Noone needed to tell me I felt I made a mistake. I knew this deep in my knowing part of my intuition. I beat myself up time and again for my mistakes. I was the hardest one on my performance and self. After all, this is my own soul's Karmic journey. In some dark recesses of my mind I felt I was failing this mission on Earth and wasted my entire twenties. However, in order to get back up on the right path I needed to pick myself back up again. This required developing a growth mindset. This transformation of a mindset is as simple as changing the narrative from "I can't do it." to " I can't do it yet." Your brain requires just a tiny tweak or rewiring to allow yourself to attune with your soul's purpose and get back on your right path. Switch from judgement and shame to curiosity and grace.

The best way to rewire your brain and start your growth mindset is to recite the Ho' oponopono Prayer. It is an ancient Hawaiian prayer. 'Ho' means to make 'opono' means "it right" and with the doubling of the phrase 'opono' means "to make it right with yourself and another". This healing prayer will release you of the resentment and judgment and bring forgiveness to yourself and the offender.

Practice **meditation** on Raven Scott Show YouTube channel. You can access the whole library in the Meditation Playlist.

- **Growth Mindset Phrases**
    1. Mistakes help me learn and grow
    2. Fall seven times, get up eight!
    3. I haven't figured it out yet.
    4. I am on the right track.
    5. I can do hard things.
    6. This might take time and effort.
    7. I stick with things and don't give up easily.
    8. I go after my dreams.
    9. I cheer myself up when it gets hard.
    10. I try new things.
    11. Learning is my superpower
    12. I focus on my own results and don't compare myself to others.

13. I was born to learn.
14. You keep going until you're proud.
15. No matter the mountain , you can climb it.
16. Challenges make you stronger.
17. You are unstoppable.
18. You follow your dreams.
19. You can choose to have a great life/(or day).
20. You are resilient.

- When It Feels Like Life Is Too Hard Or Too Much You Can...

Pause and be mindful by saying an affirmation. Meditate. Practice Gratitude. Do EFT Tapping. Do intentional breathing. Read a book. Listen to a podcast.

Pause and relax by listening to music. Splash water on my face. Breathe deeply. Listen to a book.

Pause and get outside by sitting on the porch. Go for a walk. Swim. Workout. Garden. Take your pet for a walk.

Pause and create by cleaning. Organizing. Sing a Song. Crochet. Bake. Journal. Color. Craft.

Pause and connect by calling a friend. Cuddle with a pet. Look at family photos. Have a dance party. Hug someone.

- Human Design Is A Tool For Self Discovery

The other way to jumpstart your growth mindset is knowing your soul's type, profile, center's definition, themes and purpose through your Human Design chart. Human Design is the discovery of who you are and it allows you to see the themes in your life, what you are here to do and lessons you need to learn.

Human Design will be covered thoroughly in Chapter 12, but

this brief overview will share with you why it can be so helpful in freeing you from your conditioning, expectations, of how to do and be in the world. The collective is not aware that there are these types of ways to be as human according to the Human Design theory. Not everyone is designed to as society expects. The "Just Do It" by Nike slogan that is repeated in our minds is only for 20% of the population in actuality. The industrial revolution brought about tangible systems to be productive, however we don't all operate in our best energy sources and responses in that way.

The Human Design Chart shows you if you are in alignment with your soul's purpose and motivation to make choices. If you are not aligned you are in transference and the main importance take away from Human Design is to find out what your type's strategy is in being and doing, and what your authority type is to make important decisions. We all want the secret to how to make the next right decision and your chart gives you just that.

There are certain centers in alignment with your chakras with a couple additional centers that help you know why you may struggle with a pattern. For instance as mentioned before, I am open to anyone's passions, I am easily sold an idea and easily manipulated to be on board with someone else's beliefs if I am not aware. It has taken the practice to recognize and develop my intuition knowing that I do not have to commit to anything without asking my Sacral Authority first. This felt so freeing and clear when I could ask my gut, "yes?" or "no?" and actually hear the sound of response come out of my mouth from my sacral center. I stopped writing lists, saying "yes" to commitments I didn't want to do, and I gave myself the gift of freedom to flow with intuition and what I felt called to do that day was the Divine next right choice.

On the other hand, when I feel passionate about something and believe a certain idea, I can become fixed and bull headed and, when not being wise, I judge others for not believing what I believe. This is an attribute to my defined Ajna Center. More on all the centers in Chapter 12. By learning your human design you get a really good grasp of who you are and how you can experience life aligned with your soul. It allows you to walk away from conflict that you see is not going to resolve and is causing too much negative emotions in your body. It allows you to see your areas where you can improve. It shows you the areas you may have conditioned blocks that you can exercise out. Surrendering to faith in something bigger than us, and that that power is already there within you, will help you know that you are on the right path and that you are here for a reason. Your specific strategy will help you align with Source and the energy to flow while meeting little resistance. Human Design also speaks on Intuition, and how when you can quiet your mind and allow yourself to tap into your given intuition, you will have the "Knowing" for your next right choice. You may feel like you want clarity or control over your human patterns, while that can be attained, give yourself grace that it may take your entire life time to do so and maybe even a couple thousand more. This life is a karmic journey and we are learning on Earth School in the present.

What I love about human design is that it frees us from our conditioning and opens our eyes to our uniqueness. Imagine if everyone was embraced for their uniqueness there would be world peace. It gives us a glimpse of why we are here and allows us to find our treasures within and be and act in alignment with who we truly are. We can strip off what our father expected us to believe, what our mother expected us to do, how our teachers expect us to learn, what our boss expects of our work load, and how the world expects us to act and consume.

The other concept is that our soul's journey of learning is that we are here to continually evolve, just as nature does around us. We are here to evolve our individual human experience, and we are here to evolve our community and collective systems of the world. Along with how the planets rule certain zodiac signs and energies at certain times influencing the collective energy. So do our Gates, or I call them personality traits. Some include contracts, shock, leadership, and abstraction. Each of us is here to influence the planet and collective for the betterment of our progressive movement. It is our choice to be brave and tap into that Divine Energy that is already within us.

With the five different energy types, human design recognizes that each person is like a piece of the bigger puzzle, which I've heard in Christianity as well. However there is no religion in human design. It is just a road map and information about yourself that you can utilize to make the most of your life experience now on this Earth. In our Earth village we all join our energies as pieces of that puzzle and work together to make a strong unit and balance each other out and help one another get to the end result. I believe moving forward knowing our children's human design, type and authority, will help tremendously in raising a conscious generation that will have an emotional EQ that far surpasses our current EQ. (EQ stands for emotional intelligence.) This in turn will heal our hauntings and our past, breaking ancestral patterns and rewriting subconscious unhealthy conditioning in order to bring empathy, integrity, and harmony to this Earth. How remarkable would it be to be the tiny change in the world where we're all joining together as a community to restore the Earth, be partners with Mother Nature again as our healed ancestors were.

In a world where everyone is working toward the same goal in different styles, not focusing on their own self seeking agenda, their money, and their judgemental religious ideas. Humans asleep in the matrix, grinding the pavement or in the rat race, going nowhere with your energy is wasting time and running the risk of having your immune system stressed out does not sound like a sustainable way for humans to live. The other option is we put our unique gifts together into working as a team with people that have each other's same goal and are attracted to each other with their certain energy centers and channels all magnetizing and linking. This is the super power for good moving forward in the world.

One of my treasures lost in my twenties was my musical talents and abilities. I stopped playing the piano altogether and stopped singing and writing music. One in part because I was mad at the oppressive religion and felt brainwashed, and in second part because I focused on creating a new identity.

I recently wrote a song in response to my whole journey of healing and to the treasures within. I wrote this song as a way of tapping into my old treasures that I lost and as a way to rekindle that part of me. Here are the lyrics:

Verse 1
I lost my faith on the road of life,
And on that road there was good and bad
I fell in love more than I should.
And it drove me into deceit.

Lost in the dark, trapped inside my mind.
Lost all those close who were good to me.
Absent my heart and my soul,
Oh I paid the biggest price
But...

Chorus
Now, I am free from all of it!
Unapologetic.
Never again, no more regrets
You need not to remind me.
You do not recognize me.
I found my faith, I'm coming home.
I'm coming home,
I'm coming home,
I found myself returning home.

Verse 2
Measured my worth by exterior things.
Tired of chasing love , putting on a show.
Emotions waved out of control,
Heartache wore my spirit raw.
Isolated from friends & family
My anger tried to protect my pain.
I lost that time without amends,
That I'll never regain back again.
But ...

Chorus

Bridge
We'll never know how the heavens meet the sky
And I'll never know why I had to cry.
All I know is the lessons I learned to fly.
And only when I leapt out to face my fears,
Was I able to truly cleanse my tears.

Treasure gained: Musical talents

Human Design Element affected:

I was living in my "Not Self Theme" of frustration all the time.
I suppressed my energy of my Incarnation Cross (life's purpose)
of Dominion. It was quite the opposite, I was the one being
dominated.

Dive Deeper into this topic in S3 Episode 49 How to Learn to
Radically Love Yourself & Leave a Narcissist on the Empath &
Narcissist Podcast.

- HO O' PONO PONO PRAYER

This is an ancient Hawaiin Practice that scrubs away subconscious garbage. It means "to make right - doubly right."

It is a practice of forgiveness and reconciliation first for yourself, then others. It is repentance, ie. for your subconscious ignorance. Forgiveness, ie. for being so hard on yourself. Gratitude, ie for your awareness now. And love towards yourself, innerchild, and others.

When practiced regularly, it reprograms your subconscious mind in a powerful healing way.

The Benefits help feelings of forgiveness, lowers your blood pressure, and stress, reduces depression and anxiety, and brings feelings of hope.

There is a beautiful example of how this works when Dr. Len in a Hawaiin mental illness prison cured a complete ward of criminally insane patients with this prayer without seeing any of them.

Practice this prayer and meditation on Raven Scott Show YouTube channel. You can access the whole library in the Meditation Playlist.

Transcript:

I am sorry.

Please forgive me.

Thank you.

I love you.

10. AFTERMATH OF NARCISSIST ABUSE

"**I** chose you for that very reason, you were a perfect blank canvas I could create into my own creation of a woman." I stood in shock, in disbelief. I thought, this whole eight years together I was a pawn in your game? I was your play thing? And I was dumb enough to let you!

- The highest offenders

How can one forgive someone for such an offense? They have intentionally manipulated, and harmed you through their words and with your emotions. They isolated you from loved ones and friends. They stripped you of your self worth. They are, in your mind in order to get out and stay away, enemy #1. Although my experience was traumatic for my life journey, I know others have experienced worse, and still are dealing with the narcissist through custody with a child or sibling. And it is infuriating when they defame you to your family and friends, and they believe them. The last thing you wish to do is forgive them. You are angry, and rightly so. There is a correct time for righteous anger to keep you safe and get you out of their clutches. And then as time and healing gives you freedom, there is a time for love and forgiveness.

In my deepest of conversations with Spirit I find myself resisting the feeling of letting my offender off the hook. If I forgive him, then he is allowed to get away with the offense that he afflicted on me. I will have no retribution, I will be the weak one. They should feel pain for the pain they've afflicted on me! While these are all valid points, Source does not want us to have control of this part of life. We can only control our own energies and healing. Holding onto those feelings is the same as holding in the darkness within and it poisons us and causes perpetual suffering. Every time we are reminded the darkness seeps to the surface and we are reminded of that horrible experience of how wronged we were.

How do you forgive the betrayal, and abuse? You must get to a place where you love the darkest feelings, love the seed of them, love yourself and heal through the Ho o' pono pono prayer in order for it to leave. Let go of the role of judge and punisher. If you continue to carry hatred and unforgiveness you will get sick and allow the negativity to control them. You must believe in a higher power that will distribute Karma, or retribution. You may feel sorry for the narcissist because they are so hurt and afflicted with hate and the sickness of letting the darkside take over. We are born as pure light with our souls here on Earth to learn. Those who have chosen to stray from their Earth's lessons and doing dark deeds have given in to their desires. They relish in violence, chaos, control and hate because it masks their pain. And that soul is the real sufferer. Those who forgive the offender see the child they once were and feel sadness for the pain that child experienced to end up in this realm of darkness. I do not advocate this empathy to persuade you to try and help them. And upon leaving and commencing your healing journey, you will go through a mourning process and grieve the death of a false relationship you thought was real. Nothing leaves until you love and feel the emotions that are ugly that need to come visit and be cleared. The trick for your mental health is to not ignore them or shove them inside. In order to forgive and move forward in your beautiful power, and gain freedom, you must release that pain to the Universe.

I personally found my forgiveness in learning about narcissism. Information is power, and the more I learned each layer would be removed in the gaslit perception I had of the world. Eventually years later, I reached the core of these clouded layers and discovered why I ended up in such an abusive relationship, and why it felt so familiar. My perceived loving childhood home, stunted emotional growth and self identity. I was gaslit by extreme religious ideology that any form of gaslighting felt normal. The guilt and shame was my normal mode of relating and conditioning to make sure I was a good girl, in order to feel love and acceptance. This conditioning I know wasn't malicious and not intended. It was the ancestral toxic patterns still infused in my parents' way to raise me in their "better" way. The poison and narcissism in ancestral subconscious is more powerful than our brains can ever comprehend. Until we wake up from the deep sleep of the subconscious, we then can see the "light" as clear as day. I realized that Lance was plagued with pain and lack of support he needed from his parents. He did not always feel safe and affirmed. He had to put up a hard exterior to survive his parents drama, divorce, and his violent step father's transition into the house. There were other family factors and how his father treated him that contributed as well. Not everyone who has a narcissistic parent or difficult situation grows up to be one, but his situation certainly was a recipe for it. The aftermath of his childhood trauma was, for him, he chose narcissism. The aftermath of our relationship on me was loss of friends, and family bonds, my loss of self esteem, experiencing PTSD, and having to reconstruct my life one element at a time. The aftermath of realizing I was in a narcissistic relationship lead me down a discovery that my parents were emotionally stunted to provide me the tools I needed. And as many times as I tried to share in calm conversations, drew boundaries, and even through yelling, they wouldn't absorb the information and change. Adriana Bucci stated succinctly.

> *Rational adults don't need a detailed explanation outlining that there are consequences to their actions. If your narcissistic parent can't seem to grasp or accept that abusing you throughout your entire life ended up being a HUGE deal breaker for you, you must realize that at this point in your parent's life, this isn't something you're even remotely qualified to teach to a grown adult. You also must realize they're playing dumb to escape accountability and get more supply out of you. The title of parent doesn't change what you lived through, even if no one else gets it. Keep your boundaries.*

All us humans do their best, and sometimes their best is not enough. It is a social stigma to draw boundaries with a parent and stop talking to them. I believe they are in your life to learn the ultimate lesson, not even family gets a pass for treating you poorly. In narcissistic families, abnormal is normalized. Pseudo intimacy is viewed as true connection. However, as Medium, Maria Verdeschi and I agreed on my podcast, this whole life is planned out beforehand and we must wake up to remember our lesson and make the right choices for our soul to mature. We will never know the entire plan until we find ourselves in the spirit world. All you can do is not give in to the guilt and shame and manipulative tactics, and stand in your power and make the right choice, which is usually the most difficult choice.

I was able to forgive because I saw my abuser as a child who was defenseless and scared, and there were moments together that he showed that to me, a large little child disappointed and scared. The more you work on rewiring yourself somatically, and cleansing out your negative patterns that are hardwired in you from your ancestral line, the more you grow up emotionally. We all have our inner child we carry within us. It is our job to nurture them and be our inner child's supporting parent to ourselves as we become an adult. At the end of this chapter you will practice Dealing with Difficult People Meditation, that will help you release the hate and being able to interact with them out of love and with a screen up so you are not prey to their manipulative games. This will also help you process your forgiveness. Another way I was able to heal from the aftermath was, I wrote many letters and burned them. I even wrote him an "I forgive you email", that was a mistake. Don't make contact with your past narcissist, they will take out their anger on you, even if you have the best intentions. And my spiritual self improvement journey allowed me to forgive him, myself, and others that I would find to blame. This is your journey. Each one of our scenarios and boundaries are unique. When you listen to your intuition, you will know the next right step to take in that journey. Spirit guides and our Higher Self have set up signs for us to wake up and stop to listen to the clues. Maybe it's an animal, a bell, a sound, a person, or a number on the clock. The signs are small and serendipitous. Keep an eye out and be aware, and you will recognize the signs.

-   Take Responsibility

Whatever you are not changing, you are choosing.

It is our duty in our lives to introspect into our patterns, fears, and flaws; not merely to correct them and eradicate them but to acknowledge they exist in us, in our family, and they do not have power over us. Tap into Pluto's energy, see where it is in your chart and probe deep in the mind. Ponder on where transformation needs to occur. Our life in this life is for solving mysteries, unearthing our pain and transforming it into a beautiful flower. A superpower that allows you to be strong and encouraging to others on the journey of this life. This is what I've discovered that I am here to dominate things. This is my Human Design Incarnation Cross. It has taken some time to process this and I still don't like the word. But what I believe is that I have a responsibility to share what I've learned and coach those to help them along in their journey. Dominating is my major theme of what I need to work on not doing with my ego and doing gently in the right time and space. I think the word is ironic since my whole relationship with Lance I was out of alignment and dominated by another in an unhealthy way. It's our responsibility to do the work in this lifetime and be present and conscious in every possible moment. And when we slip up, because we are not perfect, we say the Ho 'o pono pono prayer and ask for forgiveness and show vulnerability to those whom we may have affected. In doing so I relieve the suffering of others around me, and my own suffering within.

-   Spiritually Protect Yourself

We as souls are androgynous. Against popular opinion, we may have opportunities to learn through multiple lives, and we are allowed to choose the type of body we enter to help us with these lessons. As a highly task oriented soul with a past in narcissism. It was my karmic journey to experience the victim's side to learn and see how hurtful it can be.

You are here as a soulful alchemist.

Love yourself, do the mirror work, to hold space for your pain, triggers, and feelings tenderly through the darkest of times. And when you do you will transform through healing, transitions, and revelations.

You will learn to feel through life moment by moment, to trust your intuition. To trust the process. You will not know where the destination will lead you. Just as I was filled with love and encouragement by the Spirit of my Papa, you will have your Spirit Guide guide you on your journey. Feeling like an outsider gives you perspective and wisdom from generations past and the ability to look forward to strengthening your emotional intelligence to provide wise guidance moving forward and be the bridge between the past and the future breaking ancestral patterns.

I pray my pearls of wisdom have a pulse of value to you, and touch your heart. With my Human Design's Incarnation Cross being an interpersonal theme, I am aware of the impact I can make through this book, Empath & Narcissist podcast, and Workshops. You have a beautiful gift to share with the world. And I have witnessed and felt that healing allows your heart to blossom so that you can live in freedom and abundance while following the call within.

My desire for our empowering community is that it is a safe place for all to find energetic emotional alchemy and that it will empower you to find healing and balance on your unique journey. As you dive deep in your transformation, I pray you find your balance and heal both your masculine and divine feminine energy to be as circular as the yin and yang circle. I pray it holds space for you to be your most authentic you, removing your mask of social expectations and people pleasing. The Empath & Narcissist Podcast community is a container for you to learn about narcissism, to love and trust yourself, and gain back your sparkle after narcissist abuse. The workshops I created on the ravenscott.show, and via an app soon, are the safest most empowering and healing space you can guide yourself through in your own timing. The exercises and rituals allow you to alchemize your soul and transform from what you've been conditioned to be to what your true soul's identity can be. These workshops can both be a great challenge and a sacred opportunity for you on your road to healing.

May you find your soul as intimately as I have.

And remember. Always keep your unique light shining, and never let anyone else hold the pen to the story of your life.

Treasure gained: My Light & Divine Soul's Power

A Gift from Human Design & Astrology Tools:
Knowing my themes and personalities regarding areas of friends, career, partnership, money, and family in life. Discovering my strategy on how to use my energy to avoid frustration. Unveiling my life's purpose theme. Tremendous clarity on who I am, what I'm meant to do in life and how I can serve a purpose on this Earth.

Practice the Dealing with Difficult People Meditation on the next page.

Dive Deeper into this topic in Episode 68: How to Release Unconscious Patterns that Keeps the Empath Pleasing the Narcissist on the Empath & Narcissist Podcast.

- DEALING WITH DIFFICULT PEOPLE MEDITATION

Practice this **Guided meditation** on Raven Scott Show YouTube channel. You can access the whole library in the Meditation Playlist.

Transcript :

Close your eyes. Take a deep breath in. Relieve a deep breath out the mouth. Deep breath in through your nose. Same amount of breath out through your nose. Now breathe easy and relaxed.

Picture the person who is making you angry, is hurting you, is not listening to you and is difficult to resolve. See yourself staring into their eyes.

Take a deep breath in, and deep breathe out.

Now see time reverse. See this difficult person as a teenager, then as a child, then as a baby. This person was innocent and vulnerable at one point in time. This person was dependent on their mother. Now imagine them back at age six or seven. They are still vulnerable, they had hopes and dreams. They have been hurt and embarrassed. See their pain, maybe they are lonely, or ignored, or scared. This little one is inside of them still. And when their ego lashes out, know that it is their fear, their shame, and their defense mechanism.

See yourself removing some of their burdens from their arms, and assure them that they are going to be fine. You forgive them. You see them.

When it is time to see or speak to this difficult person, visualize them as a child with their fears and hold grace in your space for them. Be curious why they are saying these darts of arrows. And if they cannot soften you know you have tried your best with your ego lowered and you can draw boundaries for yourself to spend limited time with them. Maybe not talk about certain topics and pay for your own items.

Slowly take a deep breath in and a deep breath out. Wiggle your toes, flutter your eyes and arrive back in your body ready to approach this difficult person with elevated love and curiosity.

11. HEALING FROM TRAUMA

By reconnecting with yourself.

W e have reached a conclusion to know that mentally you have the power to either imprison yourself and suffer, or you can break free and have freedom, joy and a purpose filled life. It's all within your power and your mind and no matter what the circumstances are, they do not control your state of mind.

Your Emotional IQ is something that is a muscle. It is taught to be empathetic, caring, and have integrity. The more you practice your EQ and use that muscle of boundaries for yourself, and knowing when you are living in your ego versus living from your soul as light, the more you will feel connected and in the flow with your Spirit Guides, Universe, and Source. There are many ways to strengthen our emotional muscles. Here are a few that I love.

- **Gratitude**

The ability to appreciate life and how far you've come and to appreciate what you have is the practice of gratitude. It is extremely powerful and is used in the Spiritual self help world as a manifesting tool. I see it as a negative energy clearing tool. Your ego wants to protect you. Your ego is never satisfied. But your soul is grateful for the smallest of things. Start your gratitude practice by writing down every day just five things you are grateful for. At the beginning it may just be your socks, blanket, water, and air. That's ok, start with that. Continue to increase your list and write your gratitude down until you don't have anything else to list. Within a couple months work yourself up from five items to twenty five items. And go on up from there if you like. This is a daily practice that is imperative to open your mind to the joy and beauty around you. When you do that your energy will shift and other people and opportunities around you will shift in your favor. When you see the abundance of the Universe that you already have, the abundance will be like water and flow towards your open gates and bless your life with joy, love, and whatever brings you gratitude.

-   Let It Out

The most important thing to do with developing your emotional intelligence is to recognize your pain and look it straight in the eye and learn from it. To avoid the pain and shove it down and deny it exists to "stay positive" is spiritual bypassing and it will backfire on you one day in a very traumatic way. You need to get comfortable with the uncomfortable. Cry, when you need to. Write it out. Dance it out. Sing it out. Or run it out! I love this concept of writing it down and releasing it into a God box, or burning it and showering after. This practice releases and transmutes it up into the ethers, just as burning incense or a candle to say a prayer. It is subtle yet very powerful way to let it out, and is best done every Full Moon. Any way you can get all that negative energy out, do it!

It doesn't matter if anyone outside of me gets me or accepts me. I got me. I am safe.

-   **Building Self Esteem**

STOP comparing yourself to others. I know culture and school with our grading systems and magazines and movie stars make us feel conditioned to compare ourselves against the successful. This is the most unhealthy mental practice one can do. You will learn in the next chapter about Human Design and how there are thousands of variations of the system, and then you add in our personalities, with our planets in certain zodiac houses, and you have a very unique individual. Just as our fingerprints are unique and there is not one that is the same, so are our beings. We don't look at each other's fingerprints expecting them to be the same or one better than the other, they just are unique. The same should be thought of ourselves. We are unique and perfect just the way we are. This also applies to the concept of grouping certain people, cultures, and races all together, when each person in that particular culture is unique and different from the next. It is a dangerous path to assign behaviors to certain groups. Please do yourself a favor, stop doing the impossible and stop comparing yourself to the next person you see that appears successful or beautiful. The only reason our ego is comparing, is to make sure we are better than or in line with others' perceived success or beauty. This keeps us safe in the tribe. If we are doing this, more than likely we are seeking self validation and worth from sources outside yourself. When you are confident and in love with your truest unique self, you do not see life as a competition but a collaboration.

> *Stop chasing all those people who don't care about you. You look desperate and it's making you miserable. Relationships can't be forced and popularity is overrated. Focus on the people you flow with. - Mel Robbins*

-   Surrender Through Journaling

Writing down deepest feelings, honest musings, gratitude and pain is a very healthy outlet for your thoughts. They say thoughts become things. This means ideas have energy attached to them and the negative ones are toxic if they continue to swirl around in your head. So get them out! I mentioned before during a Full Moon to write out what you are feeling. Tap into when you first felt that feeling before and get it all out. The practice of incorporating all the elements is very magical about this process. The Earth, using a lead pencil, the air, the streaming of your ideas, the fire, you burn the journal entry in a safe stainless steel pot in a safe place well ventilated, and the water you shower off the energy. Why during the Full Moon? This time of the Full Moon is a time of releasing and the most potent energy the moon provides. The Moon rules our emotions, and when it is at its fullest and reflecting the Sun, which rules your identity and self, it's the perfect time to transmute it up to the Universe. You certainly do not need to wait until the Full moon to write out what you need to release. You can do this practice anytime. When you burn the journal entry, you are sacrificing those thoughts up to the Universe and allowing Source to take control of the outcome. You must shower as soon as possible to let the cleansing magic of water wash away the residual energy of your thoughts and writings.

Another wonderful practice I have found personally powerful is creating a "God box". You write down what you are struggling with and what is negative you need to express. Then fold it up, and place it in the God box. In doing this you are giving those thoughts up and letting Source take control and handle whatever needs to happen and remove the burden from your thoughts. I bought a pretty box from Michaels craft store in the back basket section. This has helped me release thoughts that if I had not surrendered, I would've stewed on and been made sick over my madness. You may also light a candle or incense and say a prayer of release when you place it in the box.

"Divine Beloved, I surrender this burden to you. You are the conductor of all. I release this worry and allow you to do what needs to be done to resolve it. I trust you in full faith. Let it be. So it is."

- **Breathe**

Pause and mindfully breathe. Place your hand on your chest and the other hand on your belly. Feel the breath fill up and thank your breath for arriving and always being there. Exhale feeling your breath empty. Again repeat, twenty times. You may play relaxing music to go along with it. Focus inwardly on your breathing and the source of your breathing. Do this in a stressful moment when you need to calm down. Do it as a daily practice during your devotional time. This returning to the mindfulness of breath brings you awareness of your life force and centers you into being aware you are purely human breathing oxygen like everyone else.

Theres too much self-centered focus. Self centered attitude is unhealthy and causes anxiety and depression. The antidote is altruism. This allows the mind to be young and at peace. Because of too much emphasis on self labels and you are isolated by yourself and more anxiety and frustration perpetuates. - Dalai Lama

- **Let It Go**

Let go of the people and things that are not serving you. This is the time you start making boundaries. You will need to write them down at the beginning and as you gain practice you will just be able to speak it. Those who repeatedly do not adhere to your boundaries or are mad with your boundaries are people you need to not chase and let go. I know this may be hard, especially if they are your parents. However, if you do not draw these boundaries you will repeatedly be uncomfortable and allow negativity in your life. Once you realize it must be done and you let them in again without the boundary, that is now your responsibility. You cannot be mad at them for offending you, because this isn't the first time. They have shown you who they are, and once you develop your muscle to stand up for yourself, the person to be mad at is yourself for not drawing the boundary. And then you can forgive yourself and know this is a learning process and set up the new boundaries to protect yourself. An example of a boundary would be not allowing someone in your sphere who is drunk, or leaving when someone is making you feel uncomfortable, or agreeing to disagree, or not allowing someone over at all.

Remember that if someone crosses your boundary there will need to be a consequence to be effective. Follow through with your consequence, so if your partner is talking down to you and not respecting you, you can ask them to stop, leave or walk away. You remove your presence and maybe that partner is not allowed in your home if they are not apologetic and continue to cross your boundaries.

If you want to see your vast potential, drop your defense and draw boundaries. - Chani Nicholas

- **Embrace Yourself**

Understand who you are and your Human Design and you will have a clear map of what your soul's authority and purpose is.

No matter how buried your treasures are, there is always hope to excavate them. The importance is to know who you are and embrace the treasures that are within you. And then you have the ability to see the patterns that are not serving you and your loved ones and change them. This is the key to your success and happiness. Investing in your self care is the way you will be able to unearth your treasures.

A couple years ago when I started on this path of spirituality rather than religion, my deceased Papa visited me in my dream. I was in a cottage with my grandma, his wife, and there was a knock on the door. I went to answer it and there was my Papa with a bright glow of light around him. He was grinning ear to ear. His words were spoken to me not through his mouth which didn't move, but through telepathy. I was shocked it was him, for in my dream I was conscious he was dead. I yelled out to my grandma, "Hey Mimi! It's Papa! He's really here!" She paid no mind. She acknowledged him, but he was there for me. He said he was so proud of me, and shared that I was on the right path. I asked if I could hug him. I missed him so much. He said "yes", and I was expecting to pass right through him and feel I was hugging air, but it was the opposite. I felt his solid mass and felt his warm comforting hug that I missed. As I hugged him, I leaned forward and found we fell through the kitchen countertop. The cottage and my grandmother were just a stage, a comfortable place for us to meet. This very well could've been my main mentor in the spirit world encouraging me on, in the suit of my Papa, or it truly could have been Papa's spirit encouraging me. Nevertheless they are one in the same. I felt that experience was so formative and tactile. I believe in our guides and the spirit world. I knew I was on the right path when I received that visit and it has given me resolve and peace of mind, no matter if anyone disagrees with me.

Believe in your experiences, stand in your truth. Because those who aim to bring you down are already below you.

Treasure gained: The right path

> Right now you feel like a neglected grapevine that appears dead outside, with no motivation to go on, and are ready to give up. Give up on hope, life , and your self worth.

> You've been kept in toxic soil with bugs eating at your roots by someone who is a parasite.

> But there is a tiny glimpse of hope.

> If and when you choose to remove yourself from the toxic soil and plant yourself in sunlight and fertile soil, to water and feed yourself through self development practices, you start to sprout a leaf, then another.

> Then all of a sudden you've transformed into a fruit bearing grapevine!!! Providing sustenance to others.

❊ ❊ ❊

> A cycle is ending a new ones beginning.

> Where souls are not putting up with the control and tyranny of others are trending.

Never again will we chase love only to be neglected.

Never again will we take the blame for their failures and defections.

Never again will they cut us down with their lies.

Never again will we be deceived by their disguise.

I'm done we're done. A cycle is ending a new has begun.

Never again will we allow their lies to prevail.

Never again will our worth be based on if we fail.

Never again will we ply and please others selfish deeds.

Never again will we snuff our light only to supply their greed.

I'm done we're done. A cycle is ending a new has begun.

I fly my white flag to the ego within. I surrender my need for Justice. I surrender my desire for revenge.

My faith in the law of Karma is strong.

I no longer believe I can fix them. I no longer care to hide their wrongs.

They say the best revenge is to release the hate, give no heed to take the bait, and heal my own self worth .

Do you dear friend believe this is true??

I believe the quest is up to you .

As for me I'm done, we're done. A cycle is ending a new
has begun.

A Gift from the Emotional Toolbox:

Gratitude Journal next page

Dive Deeper into this topic in Episode 59: How Spirit Guides
Help Empaths get Rid of Narcissists with 5 Spiritual Hygiene
Tips with Maria Verdeschi Psychic Medium on the Empath &
Narcissist Podcast.

- GRATITUDE JOURNAL

Make a daily habit of gratitude journaling. Journal about what you're grateful for and turn your narrative and turn your mindset around to be loving yourself and cheering yourself on, and realizing that you are amazing and turn your mindset around that you deserve your desires. The highest, most amazing abundance and love and blessings, is right there for you.

Grab your inspiring blank journal in our Merch shop at http://etsy.com/shop/ravenscottshow

Keep your eye out for new daily empowerment book coming in 2023.

12. HUMAN DESIGN 101

I want to state a warning. When learning any new personality type system, remember what the Dalai Lama says about self centered labels. The ego loves to organize us in tiny neat boxes. And there is a danger to using the Human Design system or any system to justify or use as a way out of self improvement and to label others. Human Design is a tool for us to gain knowledge and wisdom for how we are authentically and shows us where we can improve as a soul.

It can be an immense clarity tool that you will feel seen, heard, and validated as if the clouds are parting open.

I have learned so much about myself with the Human Design tool. Not only have I learned that I am an amplifier of people's emotions which led me to be a people pleaser, an amplifier of others' wills and drives leaving me vulnerable to every multi level scheme, and yet that I also have sharp visual intuition. I also have learned how others function. That my children have a set emotional cycle, that my husband must be quiet to properly feed his body, and that my oldest is designed as an observer rather than a doer. All of this new information allowed my ego to take a back seat, and for me to see those in my life for truly who they are and what they need. This allows you a higher perspective that stops your ego from judging others and making them do things in a way that they will not thrive.

We are all unique and process life differently. With my favorite hobby in studying astrology, I have found many correlations to client's charts and the gates and centers influence on their lives. One example is an open solar plexus and Mars being in the 12th house. Mars, the warrior and action planet in the place of secrets and subconscious imprints the energy that manifests as one hates conflict and avoids it at all costs. This also directly links to the people pleaser and the open solar plexus. One does not want feel the uncomfortable emotions of conflict because it is amplified in my body tenfold. The avoidance of conflict and bottling it up creates an intense pressure. This person will desire to relieve it, and when not released through the body with physical exercise or activities, as a result it explodes in warrior-like ways.

You may not be able to change all the details of your "flaws" all the time but knowing the areas you have been conditioned and need growth in makes you aware. And when you are aware, you are able to live in authenticity and grace.

Human Design is a freeing tool to understand yourself. Without the knowledge and roadmap you feel lost, misunderstood, abused, influenced by others and are perpetually frustrated and angry or bitter. In human design there is a term called the **non-self**, which is your existence at its lowest frequency. This leaves you operating in a mode of frustration, anger or bitterness. This appears when you are not living in alignment with your truest self and you're not in the flow with source.

Human Design was downloaded by the cosmos through Ra Uru Hu in 1987. It is not a religion, it is a road map to your personality, subconscious, themes in your life and your soul's purpose on this Earth. It combines Neutrinos, which are tiny particles of energy in our bodies imprinted by the planets' energies, Astrology, I-Ching, Kabbalah & Chakra System. You can get your chart and full audio reading provided by myself. at www.ravenscott.show/offerings. Or you can print out your own free chart at www.geneticmatrix.com or www.jovianarchive.com.

In the Human Design map you have your type of energetic body that you are, your profile, opened and defined centers, and your energetic themes in your life helping you determine your life's purpose on Earth. It's quite amazing. When I read people's charts over and over again, it confirms that their charts resonate and completely relate to their life's themes, struggles, and personalities.

I will just speak on the types here so you understand what I mean when I mention my type.

There are five types, the Generator, Manifesting Generator, Projector, Manifestor & Reflector. The Generator and Manifesting Generator make up 60% of the population and are the workers that get projects done in the world. Projectors are the worker's guides at about 20% of the population. Manifestors are the initiate and doers, but mostly initiators, at about 16% . And the Reflectors are here to gauge how humanity is feeling and being at around 4% of the population.

As a mother I will give you the perspective of the types of children's needs and you will see it in yourself as well. For example, I am a **Generator**. I have energizer bunny energy, I can do and do and do and love accomplishing projects. As children us generators love to work on projects, but only the projects we are interested in. I remember procrastinating on school projects I did not want to do. We have a tendency to rebel, because you just can't tell us what to do! We make lots of rude noises, and that's actually our authority, unless you have a defined solar plexus. We are supposed to make a noise from our sacral, the gut, of a "uh hu" for yes. "Uh uh" for no. and "hmmm" for maybe. This is the sacral authority. So we have been conditioned to ignore our sacral noise because it's rude to use that noise! We were taught to "Use our words. Please" It's ok they didn't know. Wink wink.

Manifesting Generators have a lot of independence, are master multitaskers, and don't like to slow down to explain things. They "know already" but also tend to skip steps because they are trying to get the end result they envision too fast. This type of child will have an idea to go play at the neighbors house, and just go without telling you because it takes too much time. They wander back and get in trouble because their mother has been "worried sick about them." They have a combo of both energies of Generator and Manifestor so those apply to this child too. Sorry it's like parenting three children at once. I have one so I understand the struggle.

Projectors are observers. These children don't do long tasks well, therefore long days at school are extremely exhausting and I've found relaxing in bed one hour before bedtime with lights out or low aids in a restful sleep. They have spurts of energy to do work, and need lots of play time and breaks. Every child benefits with this format because they learn through play, however, this child needs it. They are here to learn through observation and need to be exposed to lots of new concepts and things to observe. They are ultimately here to guide the doers, the above generators and manifesting generators. They will burn out if you force them to work long hours as the "workers" are designed to do. This child needs to be recognized and asked for their opinion for them to align with their true selves. Projector children need to be recognized and listened to. They have lots of great ideas since they are constantly perceiving the world. Ask them what their ideas are before they are bugging you to no end to share them. They will feel heard and seen and your relationship will grow stronger.

Manifestors are here to envision and initiate projects. They also do not have longevity for work so these children do best working in spurts and time to play. They are naturally survivors and self-directed so they can be very challenging. It's extremely important for this child to inform adults and adults to empower them by giving them choices. So ask, would you like broccoli or banana? This helps with all children but you will hit less resistance with this child.

Reflectors need consistency and do not transition easily. Because they have open Spleen and Identity Centers they will be clingy to the parent. They need to feel good in their environment since they are reflecting everyone else's energy centers. If they don't feel good they need to be free to move or leave. You may need to move them around a bit until they find a place that feels good to them. They amplify everyone else's energy so if they are near a child with alot of fear or sadness they won't feel good and need to move to a more calm child who is sure of themselves. They do like to be in school, but will feel the energy if there is unrest and complain. Be careful which friends they have since they reflect and amplify their friends feelings and energies. In the teen years this is important they don't hang out with the wrong crowd.

Now that you've seen how these types are as children you can interpret that in the grown up world.

Generators are the worker bees, great employees getting tasks done. Manifesting Generators are always working on new projects and multitasking. They are also great employees, yet like to start new projects and are independent. Projectors are amazing counselors and teachers as they have observed everything and are excellent at relaying what they've learned. Manifestors are great start ups or owning their own company's with their major vision and need for support in employees and worker bees to carry the energy for their ideas. Reflectors are excellent coaches or therapists with a real understanding for how people feel, they are also great doctors as Projectors can be and other types with the mind of a scientist. These are all generalities and anyone can be what they want. The trick is to follow your strategy and authority in making choices as you move through life.

- **Strategy - The Key To Living In The Flow.**

Generator : Wait to respond. This is the hardest strategy of all, especially for this body full of energy. The best I can describe how to wait is to wait for whatever energy to lead you into action. Be mutable, flow like water. When you wake don't go off a list, feel out what is right for the day to get done. When you do so your mojo will flow. Also you can respond to people reaching out. You can respond to intuition, say you hear a small voice to call a friend. You don't have to wait for a big truck to drive by, life is in the little small energy wavelengths. Big life changes are required to wait to respond. Pushing to initiate will only bring you blocks and frustration.

Manifesting Generator: Envision, inform, and wait to respond. This is a mixture of the "doer" Generator, and the "visionary" Manifestor. You get to dream and create and it is very important to inform the Universe and/or others of your vision so that Source will bring you someone or something to respond to in relation to your vision. Do what you love while you wait, plan, sketch, dream, plan and then you will have all the tools to pull the trigger once someone reaches out to you and says "I have been thinking about" - fill in the blank and you will have their solution! they are mega creative and move at the speed of light, if they skip a step, it's important to remember not to beat themselves up, and embrace their non linear creative process.

Projector: Wait to be invited. Projectors live their most aligned when they wait to be asked for their sage advice. As observers they have a wealth of wisdom, however their advice seems bossy and is not welcome when offered without the other asking. Don't worry if you are one, you will be asked by the people who will receive your advice with your magnetic aura. They have an energetic aura that probes and those who need their help will feel compelled to ask. Projectors do not have energy centers so they need to reprogram themselves to not just push through and do it. Waiting for the next big invitation is what they are designed for, not lazy. When in the flow they will subconsciously study about something they will be invited into. Major life changes you must wait for the invitation, love, marriage, career, moving, or traveling. If they initiate they will experience struggles.

Manifestor : Inform and take action. This is the only type that the "just do it" slogan applies. Envisioning how your action will impact others involved is the key to a wise and powerful Manifestor. Telling these others is important so they know what to expect and then they will experience little to no resistance while executing their plan. This may sound simple enough, but Manifestors do not like to stop and inform others due to childhood programming and people stopping them based on their fears and limitations. However, know that just because they have informed them does not mean you have to change or stop if they do not understand what you are doing. Just letting people know what to expect is all you have to do. This is not a one way street, Manifestors love when others share what they are doing as well and it forms a trust bond that can create peace, love and flow.

Reflector : Wait 28 days to make a major life decision. Your energy is lunar; maybe that's why you love her (Luna) so! They are open centered beings absorbing energies all around. This brings consistent change and they need time to decide that this major life change is their own and not from an outside energy. Spend quality meditation time to reflect on what is your true internal and not external opinion or influence. I know this can be frustrating in these demanding times to go and do, however if you do not you will experience disappointment.

- **Centers**

The centers are places in your body that carry energy frequencies and contain the gates that define your personality. They coincide with the Chakras with a couple added in. If you have a center colored in on your chart that is defined and that is your steadfast energy. If it is white and open then you amplify other defined people's energy around you. And are more prone to exterior forces and conditioning in those centers.

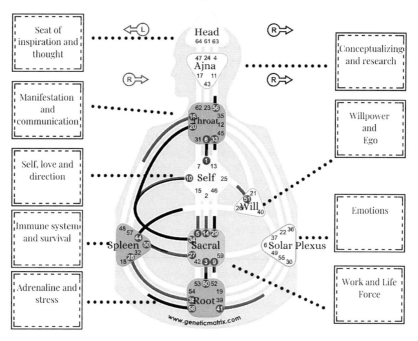

Head - Inspiration : This Center is the seed of thought. It is where you receive intuitive thoughts, inspiration, and receive messages from Source.

- Open (uncolored) An open head has a flood of ideas
- Defined (colored yellow) The defined Head center is one that is the inspirational force of the Earth, their head is always "on", and active. They require lots of food to fuel their active brain and typically have a fast metabolism.

Ajna - Conceptualization : This Center is the location of conceptualization. Where inspiration forms into thought, plans, and concepts. The place where the hypothesis, research, and conclusion all are formed.

- Open (uncolored) An open ajna has a whole number of concepts it is processing, the downside to this is these centers don't have the energy to follow through and finish and are easily distracted.
- Defined (colored green) The defined Ajna center holds fast to ideas and is a bit judgmental of other ideas, on the flip side it is trustworthy and reliable.

Throat - Manifestation & Communication : This Center is the location of language, communication and manifestation. Since words become things, speaking creates movement. What we speak about is directly connected to the defined gates in the throat and what other centers it is connected to. This center is a *motor*.

- Open (uncolored) An open throat is a talker, they feel uncomfortable in the silence and feel pressure to fill the gap with empty conversation.
- Defined (colored brown) The defined throat center speaks with consistency and authority, is best when asked, and may hold back if others are speaking.

G/Self Identity - Self, Love, Direction : This center is the location of self, love and one's compass. This is the place where the soul is seated. This center is where you understand who you are.

- Open (uncolored) The open G center feels how other's sense themselves, this allows for great empathy and understanding to help others as a counselor, however this also can lend for outside influences to easily turn someone into a sweet rule follower to a rebellious rule breaker if they are in the wrong crowd.
- Defined (colored yellow) The defined G/Self Center is self confident, and is here to give love.

Will - Will Power, Ego : This center is a *motor*, and governs value, business, and energy to be motivated to get things done. This is where you have the power to sell someone on your idea or be sold on another's idea. The motivation to diet, exercise, start a business, start a project, do your chores, and so on.

- Open (uncolored) The open Will center influences those who amplify and are easily sold on someones' enthusiastic idea or product, the downside to this is you may find your house full of multilevel marketing products and a few days later not really want them at all.
- Defined (colored red) The defined Will center is stubborn, yet self motivated and determined.

Sacral - Life Force : This center is a *motor* and is where your being resides. This is where the work force comes from and life force comes from.

- Open (uncolored) The open sacral is a person who needs lots of breaks and may appear lazy, they do not have the defined motor and need the collective to help get projects and things done, if they try to keep up with those who have the motor defined they will burn out.
- Defined (colored red) The defined Sacral Center is your energy motor for doing. This is the battery for doing. You need to exhaust your motor daily, so be creative, working and exercising a bunch for you to sleep well at night.

Spleen - Awareness, Immune System : This center holds your intuition, has influence on timing, lymph nodes and the immune system. It is all about survival. You know when you ignore your gut and do it anyway and then regret it later? Yes this is what the spleen center governs. Our fear gates reside in the spleen center to keep us safe, and sometimes limit us from our dreams. They are not permanent. The fears come and go in the moment so you can learn to recognize them and evaluate if they are a fear for survival or a fear that can be pushed through for a breakthrough.

- Open (uncolored) The open spleen is sensitive to fear, and a sensitive immune system, however they can feel if they are coming down with a cold and rest to catch it. They feel safe and secure with someone with a defined spleen center.
- Defined (colored brown) The defined Spleen Center is highly intuitive and can sense good and bad people and situations. This has a strong immune system, however they are not sensitive to symptoms, so may plow through and be taken down badly by a cold. The defined spleen person is all about the now, and acting in the now is a survival technique.

Solar Plexus - Emotion : This center governs our emotions. It is a *motor* center and this emotional energy fluctuates in cyclical waves.

- Open (uncolored) The open solar plexus provides a person with great empathy for how others feel, however they also can be people pleasers due to not wanting to amplify the other's negative emotions.
- Defined (colored brown) The defined Solar Plexus has a consistent wave of emotions, high, mid, low and back high again. Because you experience emotions in a wave it would be clever to keep a diary of your emotions and see the cycle. It is also important for you to honor yourself and understand that this is a process and your authority. To find the stillness in your emotions is the key to making important decisions. It will never serve you to make decisions at the top or bottom of your emotion cycle.

Root - Adrenaline, Stress : This center governs the adrenaline. This center influences one to be obsessively motivated to get things done or cyclically motivated to get things done. This is a pressure center pushing up to the sacral motor of the workforce.

- Open (uncolored) The open root center is one who gives

you constant needless pressure to get to-do lists done, they are positive if they get on work and projects right away because they feel the urgency to do so. How do your open centers affect your frustrations?

- Defined (colored brown) The defined Root Center is another cyclical energy for motivation. When the cycle is up the energy is up too and when the cycle is low the energy for urgency is non existent. They take their time in moving forward with anything unless they are really passionate about it. How do your defined centers affect your themes.?

In my human design readings I use the acronym *TREASURE* to help people figure out who they are based on finding out their gifts, talents within, and the reason your soul is here. Your character traits, themes, and life purpose are all incorporated in the human design system.

T : Traits : Your character traits can be explained through your gates & channels. They give words and reasons to your themes that continue to occur, good and bad. I call the gates traits. These are energies that you hold that are expressed as character traits. You have many defined in your chart, and they align with a planet and it's energies. You can learn a lot about yourself and recognize in your chart that you resonate with the gate (trait). You may have it labeled red as your unconscious trait which is what we do not normally recognize but others in our life do. And you have the labeled black as your conscious traits that your mind is aware of. You may have "hanging gates", those are the numbers circled in red and then only half of the white channel filled in red or black. If you have a gate defined with a red and black line, that is a reinforced trait in your subconscious body and conscious mind.

You will find your partner and friends have the other half of some of your gates so when you are together you complete an energetic circuit. We are all pieces to a larger puzzle.

A number connected to another number with full red/ black is called a channel. These circuits are all very unique and specific to it being an individual energy, tribal energy for the group you are surrounded by, or a collective energy for the greater whole such as systems and infrastructure.

In a reading you will receive information about your traits, and your channels. These help you understand yourself better, enforce you are on the right path, and shed light on where your focus should be.

I think it is important to look at the illustrations on the next page to see what your gates are activated to talk about and which fears are activated. When you are caught up in your ego's agenda these fears will ignite and hinder your progress. The key is the push through the fear and you will find rewarding results.

Recognition is the first step to healing.

Fear about

48. being inadequate
or not ready
57. the future or of the
unknown
44. repeating the
mistakes of the past
50. failing your
responsibilities
32. failure
28. that life is empty
and meaningless
18. you are not perfect
or nothing is perfect

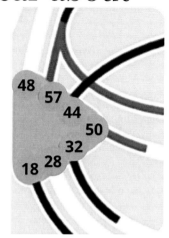

Discovering Treasures Within

Speak about

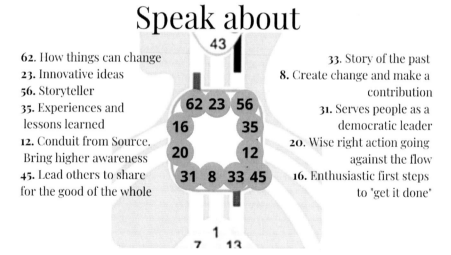

62. How things can change
23. Innovative ideas
56. Storyteller
35. Experiences and
lessons learned
12. Conduit from Source.
Bring higher awareness
45. Lead others to share
for the good of the whole

33. Story of the past
8. Create change and make a
contribution
31. Serves people as a
democratic leader
20. Wise right action going
against the flow
16. Enthusiastic first steps
to "get it done"

Discovering Treasures Within

R: Raised influences : R is for raised conditioning and the energy you are open to outside influences. These are referring to your open centers. Centers are the shapes on your chart. They are aligned with the chakra system. See the chart for which shape is which center. When you think about an open center, it can always be for good or can be a challenge just as in every element in life. The benefit for a center being open is you have empathy in that center and can feel others' energies. The open is an amplifier of others.

E: Engrained : The colored in shapes mean they are defined. They are a natural solid part of your energy that does not waiver from outside influences. These have their pros and cons as well.

A: Authority : How to best learn how to use your authority in making decisions. Pure Authority means one needs to listen to their guttural sounds. Emotional Authority are those with a defined Solar Plexus center and need to find the middle of the curve in their emotions to make decisions, wait until the choice feels right. Splenic Authority has an intuitive pulse in the moment, trust your gut and act on it.

S: Strategy : Your strategy is how you can live aligned in your life. How to take action, how to manifest, and how to attract your dreams. Each type has its own strategy

U: Understanding you - **Profiles:** These are how you move through life as a theme. Your overall energy is another way to describe it, or your patterns you continue to find yourself in.

Line 1 is Investigator: This is someone who needs to know everything about a topic, trip, venture, etc. They are the planners. They will know about all the best local places to eat and stay for a trip due to their research. They will gather all the information before making a decision. They either need to know everything all the time. And sometimes have so much going on they are fine with it being on a need to know basis. As a child, they would ask 100 questions, read all the books on one topic, and want to get as much hands-on learning about that topic as possible. They might read an encyclopedia for fun.

Line 2 is the Hermit: This theme is pretty much as it sounds. They can be social, however are very comfortable in their own space hunkered down in their "cave". They do not venture out much, and don't do change well. They are perfectly content living in the same location their whole life. They do not like to be bothered with errands. And have to be pulled out of their shell and out into the social scene. But once they are they are quite a powerful friend. This child doesn't do transitions well and needs five minute warnings before leaving, cleaning up, or moving on to the next activity. If they don't they will fight you about the transition and throw a fit.

Line 3 is the Martyr: This book illustrated a perfect example of a 3 Line Martyr. They go through life through trial and error. They don't ever make a mistake in life, they just learn from that experience. My sister loved to learn lessons and found herself as a child getting in trouble for it. But she couldn't help it, her main Profile is a 3 of the Martyr. This just meant she had to try it even if she was told no. She thrived on trial and error to learn the outcome as the ultimate scientist. Her jumping into motherhood at such a young age is another example of learning through experience. She grew and adapted through the process. This is why a tight rein on this type of child will drive a wedge between your relationship. This type of person will have no problem and will gladly share with you their experiences and lessons and how to NOT do something.

Line 4 is the Opportunist: This person is full of drive towards opportunities. For social friends, career, or projects. They value community and love their close ones deeply. They are all about bringing the resources together for the village. They would be good business people, always coming up with brilliant ways to make money. They are capable of adapting in each social setting to network and make friends for new opportunities. This child would be outgoing, witty, a class leader and have charisma. They do not do well when they are betrayed in their trust, and they can become half-hearted, mean or withdrawn. They need to be reminded to open up to life and live again. This child will need reminding that not everyone is perfect.

Line 5 is the Heretic: This energy is constantly coming up with ideas and conceptualizing everything. This energy can make a great leader and guide. They do however need constant reality checks so they can balance their fantastical imagination. Children with this line may daydream, but have an expansive imagination.

Line 6 is the Role Model: This energy is typically the natural leader. They tend to feel responsible all the time. They may need time alone so not to feel on demand for the responsibility. But then they can't help themselves take charge because they are born to take charge. They need to learn to release the pressure to be responsible for everything and ask for help. Finding a team to delegate to and help support this person would be helpful for their stress level. Children with this need to be coached to relax, have fun and not worry about being so serious. It can be tempting to encourage more responsibility within them, but they already have a great deal of pressure, so giving them time to dance, laugh and play is very important.

R: Reason you are here - **Incarnation Cross** : This is the most magical part of the Human Design chart. It gives you your life's main theme and lesson of what you are here to learn! How cool is that?! The searching is over. It will not spell it out exactly. It is an energetic theme. However once you are aware it becomes a beacon of light to guide you in your spiritual and life journey. It gives you permission to be your unique self. And it helps you understand others once you learn their type, and incarnation cross. This carnation, i.e. lifetime, is for you to learn this theme in your chart. There are many unique themes for each person, a reading of your chart done by myself will give you a beautiful description from a special book The Book of Destinies. Plus I will pull your Natal Astrology chart and share your North Node Guidance to combine the two and give you a clear and powerful purpose to focus on. This is the best way to discover your Destiny. You can book a free exploratory call and purchase your Reading at www.ravenscott.show/offerings

E: Energy type - Generator, Manifestor, Manifesting-Generator, Projector, or Reflector as described above.

All of these elements are what make up your human design and road map to knowing yourself.

- **What if?**

What if we taught our children at a young age what their authority is and how they can make decisions? What their type is and how to apply their strategy? We would stop trying to fit a square into a round hole. They would grow up confident, emotionally intelligent, aligned, and in the flow of their life's purpose. They wouldn't feel so lost. Who knows? Maybe less suicides would occur. Maybe less violence or self harm and hurting occur. They would grow up and create a society that works together as a team and pieces to a puzzle rather than doing it all alone and burning out.

There would be less heartache, less pain, less regrets, less buyer remorse, less debt, less people pleasing, less self sacrificing, and less emotional suffering and more self sovereignty.

Dive Deeper into this topic in S3 Episode 31: How to Decondition yourself with Human Design Strategy on the Empath & Narcissist Podcast.

Acknowledgements

I want to express my gratitude for everyone who has helped me and helped this book come to fruition. First I have to thank my supportive partner and family. Without their support I would not have had the courage to share.

I thank the support of my friends Jessica Mroz, Kristy Martin, and Vilma Recchiuti for encouraging me to press on and write this book, and for supporting me as I hit imposter syndrome and walls. Without their cheerleading this book would be dead in the water.

I want to thank Anthony Nwaneri of AT Publishing for giving me advice on my cover and title. It's not every day you meet a kind stranger who wants to help you with nothing expected in return.

I wondered for so long why I fell for the trap and ended up in an abusive relationship with someone who didn't truly care about me. But now I know. It's a karmic journey to see the other perspective, to gain experience and to deepen my empathy for those who need coaching and help. I am grateful to my x for all the life experiences and lessons we went through together and I what I allowed myself to endure to make me wiser and stronger.

And of course I thank my husband for always holding space for my meltdowns, growth and healing. And being that strong root bringing me clarity and the harsh truths I needed to hear to change my patterns and evolve. I have loved you for a thousand years, and will love you for a thousand more.

About The Author

Raven Scott is a survivor of a narcissitic abusive relationship. She is a certified meditation teacher and Human Design Reader. She teaches you how to stop the stress cycle, heal from your pain and trauma, and reinvigorate you to get your sparkle back and redesign your life. She talks direct and shares how to jump off the crazy train of toxic relationships, draw boundaries, how to find your voice and inner lionheart.

She is an international role model, spiritual mentor, the co-author of Discovering Life's Journey written *by Vilma Recchiuti* and author of Empath & The Narcissist, and host of The Raven Scott Show on NA TV Network and her own channel on YouTube. And executive producer and host of Empath & The Narcissist Podcast. She discovers her clients' unique soul's blueprint through Human Design and North Node focus Astrology readings. She delivers girl talk for seekers focusing on healing & renewal, breaking ancestral patterns and creating their dream life through spirituality and practical methods. She has created her book to help empower and inspire others to break the negative patterns that do not serve them and discover their treasures within.

With personal experience of being her family's black sheep, she has embraced her solo path and dominates breaking toxic ancestral patterns.

She is an Ambassador of regain your sparkle back after narcissist abuse. And mentor helping empaths heal from their black sheep wound through her transformational workshops.
Through grounded and heart centered teachings she elevates the spiritual journey and concepts that you are uniquely magnificent and contrary to your doubts, you are here for a purpose.

Her unique approach to addressing the souls journey v the ego's protection mode, gives men and women hope and clarity of their themes they are meant to grow from.

As an international author, narcissist abuse recovering coach, Podcast host of Empath & Narcissist and creator of Narcissistic Abuse Recovery workshop. She is dispelling the narcissist power one soul at a time.

She has created a companion workshop, a FREE How Empaths Can Draw Powerful Boundaries. You can download and start your transformation today! https://ravenscott.show/free-workshop

Follow her on YouTube, at Raven Scott Show . Listen to her podcast Empath and The Narcissist on Apple, Spotify or anywhere you listen to your podcasts.

If you like this book and Raven, be sure to write a review on Amazon. Find out how you can dive deeper with her at http://ravenscott.show

YouTube: http://youtube.com/channel/UC7aia23E-LDXhZobUmzTcgg
Medium: http://medium.com/ravenscottshow
Podcast: http://ravenscott.show
IG: http://instagram.com/ravenscottshow
Twitter: http://twitter.com/ravenscottshow
Email: ravenscottshow@gmail.com

Healing tools

Access full Guided Meditation Library at : Raven Scott Show YouTube Channel/ Meditation Playlist

https://youtube/channel/UC7aia23E-LDXhZobUmzTcgg

Discover the App: Recover with Raven
coming in December 2022

Chapter 1:

- Conscious Parenting

- Astrology for Self Discovery

- Parenting Manifesto Journal

Chapter 2:

- Guided Shadow Work

Chapter 3:

- Emotional Release Painting Exercise

Chapter 4:

- Inner Child Meditation

Chapter 5:

- Empath Protection Meditation

- Inner Authority Mantra

Chapter 6:

- Drawing Boundaries

- Chakra Healing Meditation

- Mirror Work Part 1

- Dream Journal

Chapter 7:

- EFT Tapping

- Removing Dark Energy

Chapter 8:

- Mirror Work Part 2

- Connect to Healed Ancestor Meditation

Chapter 9:

- Ho o' pono pono Prayer

Chapter 10:

- Dealing with Difficult People Meditation

Chapter 11:

- Gratitude Journal

Chapter 12:

Human Design 101

[1] Caligor, Eve; Levy, Kenneth N.; Yeomans, Frank E. (May 2015). "Narcissistic Personality Disorder: Diagnostic and Clinical Challenges". *The American Journal of Psychiatry*. Washington, D.C.volume=172: American Psychiatric Association (5): 415–22.

Diagnostic and Statistical Manual of Mental Disorders: DSM-5 (5th ed.). Washington, D.C.: American Psychiatric Publishing. 2013. pp. 645, 669–72. ISBN 9780890425558.

[2] Return to Calm

Manufactured by Amazon.ca
Acheson, AB